TECHNOLOGY

FOR TEACHERS

MASTERING NEW MEDIA
AND PORTFOLIO
DEVELOPMENT

Joseph H. Howell
Pensacola Jr. College

Stephen W. Dunnivant
Gulf Coast Community College

Boston   Burr Ridge, IL   Dubuque, IA   Madison, WI   New York   San Francisco   St. Louis
Bangkok   Bogotá   Caracas   Lisbon   London   Madrid
Mexico City   Milan   New Delhi   Seoul   Singapore   Sydney   Taipei   Toronto

McGraw-Hill Higher Education

A Division of The McGraw-Hill Companies

TECHNOLOGY FOR TEACHERS:
MASTERING NEW MEDIA AND PORTFOLIO DEVELOPMENT

This book is printed on acid-free paper.

1 2 3 4 5 6 7 8 9 0 DOC/DOC 0 9 8 7 6 5 4 3 2 1 0

ISBN 0–07–235547–6

Editorial director: *Jane E. Vaicunas*
Sponsoring editor: *Beth Kaufman*
Editorial coordinator: *Teresa Wise*
Marketing manager: *Daniel M. Loch*
Editing associate: *Joyce Watters*
Senior production supervisor: *Mary E. Haas*
Coordinator of freelance design: *Michelle D. Whitaker*
Senior supplement coordinator: *David A. Welsh*
Typeface: *11/14 Comic Sans & Gill Sans Ultra Bold*
Printer: *R. R. Donnelley Sons Company/Crawfordsville, IN*

Freelance cover designer: *Jamie O'Neal*
Cover image: © *Comstock Stock Photography*

www.mhhe.com

Table of Contents

Table of Contents (continued)

Topics of Study (continued)

Table of Contents (continued)

Appendices (continued)

Technology for Teachers

Preface

You now hold in your hands one of the most unique approaches to teacher education in recent years. Don't put this book down until you've read this preface and given the CD-ROM a quick review! If you are interested in teaching, or are currently teaching, you will immediately see how this project differs from so many others. *Technology for Teachers: Mastering New Media and Portfolio Development* is more than another compilation of theory and practice. This workbook and companion CD-ROM combine to immerse the student in the continuum of educational technology integration. Technology in today's classroom must move beyond computer literacy and business applications (word processors, spreadsheets, and databases). It must become more than computerizing examinations and purchasing the latest educational software. Technology must become a normal tool for daily instruction, so well integrated into teaching and learning that it becomes the "tool of choice" for teachers.

Technology for Teachers: Mastering New Media and Portfolio Development guides you in a self-education process that models the best of teaching and learning. The CD-ROM provides access to valuable articles and presentations exploring key topics of educational technology and links to Internet-based archives of information. As you explore the various educational technologies, your journey will be recorded in a portfolio workbook. This creation will serve you long after the coursework is completed, providing an archive of self-reflected knowledge from which to build exciting lessons and manage 21st century classrooms.

If you want to be a successful teacher (or if you are already one), you realize that integrating technology into instruction is not a goal, but a journey. The life of today's teacher is complex — you must design quality lessons, make informative, and hopefully exciting, presentations, and manage a classroom of challenging students. To accomplish this, you are called to create rich environments for activity-based instruction, to find authentic means of measuring student learning, and to report student progress in an easy-to-understand way to your supervisors and parents. In short, if you want to survive as a teacher, you must become a resourceful, reflective artist of learning, providing enlightening and entertaining learning opportunities for your students.

An emerging paradigm in education rejects the passive instruction of the past and calls for active learning on the part of engaged students with assessment driving instructional design. You heard right: designing effective learning opportunities begins with assessment. We need to know what we will measure and how we will measure it before we begin teaching. Even further, the best assessment occurs within the act of instruction, not as an isolated entity. These qualities of the "new teaching and learning cycle" are at the very core of all activities in the *Technology for Teachers: Mastering New Media and Portfolio Development* workbook and CD-ROM.

Materials Design and Integration

The *Technology for Teachers: Mastering New Media and Portfolio Development* includes a student portfolio workbook and companion CD-ROM. These two resources work in tandem. Each section on the CD-ROM contains informative articles on selected topics of educational technology and instructional design. Each section begins with key articles on these topics, accompanied by extended resources available through a "live" Internet connection. After interacting with these materials, students complete activities in the workbook and on the CD-ROM. These activities, and the resulting portfolio "artifacts," provide students with "firsthand" experience in authentic learning and assessment.

Scholars of educational assessment argue that three levels of "evidence" are required to adequately measure student learning: (1) traditional concrete knowledge acquisition, (2) knowledge constructs and reflection, and (3) knowledge transfer and performance. Together, these three form a "triangle of evidence" of student progress. This multidimensional approach to assessment stands in contrast to traditional "directed" learning and assessment that focus almost exclusively on factual knowledge and objective testing. The "triangle of evidence" extends assessment to higher-order thinking and the performance of "real-world" skills. This workbook strives to address each side of the "triangle of evidence" when assessing learning.

Each section of the workbook and CD-ROM includes opportunities for you to become familiar with key terms and answer traditional questions. In addition to these traditional activities, innovative exercises require students to engage the content of the section and produce a "learning product" relevant to that topic. These activities require work in collaborative groups of varying sizes, research on effective practices, evaluation of instructional technology models, and much more. Finally, at the end of each section, students reflect on what they have learned and experienced in both structured and open journals. These reflection journals are typed into Web forms for easy printing. Collectively, all of these learning exercises constitute the student's learning portfolio. At the conclusion of the course, students will have a robust body of work to include in a resume and, more importantly, to refer to as they enter a teaching career.

The key to this portfolio building is the *Technology for Teachers* CD-ROM. This easy-to-use tool requires no special installation. Simply launch your Web browser (i.e., Netscape Navigator or Microsoft Internet Explorer) and follow the instructions in the following section. As you navigate the simple menus of the CD-ROM, keep in mind that some links lead to "on-board" materials (actually on the CD), while others link to external Web sites and require a "live" Internet connection. As you explore and complete each section of the workbook, be sure to archive all of your notes and exercises. You might consider placing these materials and the workbook in a separate three-ring binder or appropriate folder. Your course instructor may have additional instructions for you to follow. Regardless of the way you save your work, be bold in your projects. Explore new territory. Ask challenging and provoking questions in class. Create controversy and foster disagreement. Never overlook the importance of the obvious. Question the use of technology. Above all, be frank and unreserved in your reflections. These writings will serve as the foundation for making you a reflective teacher.

Quick Installation Guide

Microsoft Internet Explorer 4.0 and 5.0

1) Insert the CD-ROM into your CD-ROM drive.

2) Launch Internet Explorer (from your "Start" menu in Windows 95 or your taskbar in Windows 98).

IMPORTANT: You do not have to connect to the Internet to browse the contents of the CD-ROM.

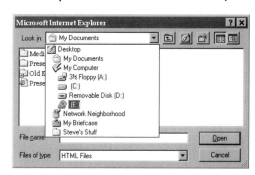

3) After Internet Explorer starts, click the "File" command.

4) Select "Open."

5) Click the "Browse" button.

6) Browse to your CD-ROM drive.

7) Double click your CD-ROM drive letter.

8) Locate and select the file labeled "index.htm."

9) Click "Open," then "OK."

10) Your Web browser should now display the home page of the CD-ROM. From here, you can easily access all resources on the CD by following the links.

Netscape Communicator/Netscape Navigator 4.0

1) Insert the CD-ROM into your CD-ROM drive.

2) Start Netscape Navigator from your "Start" menu.

IMPORTANT: You do not have to connect to the Internet to browse the contents of the CD-ROM. Click "File," then "Go Offline" if you do not wish to be connected while you browse the CD-ROM.

3) After Netscape starts, click the "File" command.

4) Select "Open Page." Make sure the "Navigator" radio button is marked.

5) Click the "Choose File" button.

6) Use the "Open" dialog box to browse to your CD-ROM drive.

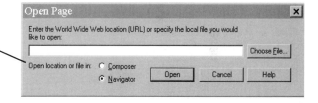

7) Double click your CD-ROM drive letter.

8) Locate and select the file labeled "index.htm."

9) Click "Open," then click "Open" again.

10) Your Web browser should now display the home page of the CD-ROM. From here, you can easily access all resources on the CD by following the links.

Macintosh   System 7.5 and Higher

1) Insert the CD-ROM into your CD-ROM drive.

2) An icon will appear on your desktop.

3) Double click the CD-ROM icon

4) Locate the file labeled "index.htm" in the CD-ROM folder.

5) This should start your default Web browser and load the home page of the CD-ROM. From here, you can easily access all resources on the CD by following the links.

> **NOTE:**
> This CD-ROM requires installation of a Web browser and the Adobe Acrobat Reader. If you do not have this software installed on your computer, see the instructions in "Appendix I: Installing Additional Software Tools" to install these software tools from the *Technology for Teachers* CD-ROM.

Teacher's Guide

We're very excited to bring you *Technology for Teachers: Mastering New Media and Portfolio Development*. This portfolio workbook and companion CD-ROM will provide your students with opportunities to explore new technologies, design effective learning environments, and practice an array of skills needed to become successful teachers. Each section of the CD-ROM contains activities designed to motivate and engage the learner while addressing areas of critical need for tomorrow's educators. Each section also contains a project based upon the topic within that section. Students are asked to respond to relevant questions for each area and share their general reflections on the topic of study. We recommend that you have students place all of their work and the workbook in a three-ring binder. This convenient gathering of portfolio materials will allow you to evaluate student progress throughout the course.

Strategies for Success

Facilitate learning through classroom discussion.

Create an atmosphere of trust where students can express their thoughts.
> Conversations in a trusting atmosphere can create memorable moments of learning!

Empower your learners by encouraging their creativity.

Model your best teaching strategies.
> You are, after all, their role model.

Encourage questions and arguments and foster disagreements to engage learners.

Incubate reflection.
> Reflective teachers must first become reflective learners.

Stress assessment over all else as the cornerstone of design.
> How can we design lessons without knowing how we will measure their effectiveness?
> Consider using the student portfolio as the sole measure of student achievement.
> Performance is the assessment!

When you cover theory, put it into action.

Share your successes in the classroom (and your failures).

Practical Recommendations

We encourage you to take time to explore the contents of the CD-ROM and the online materials and resources. As you preview each section, keep in mind that you are one of the learners in the process. Don't be afraid to explore a particular topic in more depth or recommend additional activities for students. You may be confronted with an area of unfamiliar technology. Use this situation to learn with your students. When you find a learning moment in the classroom, seize it! Allow students to pursue topics of individual interest. Be comfortable with the fact that you don't have all the answers, especially when it comes to technology. While technology gives students the freedom to explore the world, it's up to you to make this a worthwhile and enjoyable journey.

Learner's Guide

So you want to be a teacher. That's great! Now all you have to do is learn how to manage a classroom full of eager students using the latest technologies that are guaranteed to keep them on the edge of their seats. No problem, as long as you realize that your preparation for this exciting career begins now. That's right, you start your career as an educator today. *Technology for Teachers: Mastering New Media and Portfolio Development* presents you with a unique opportunity to create and explore educational technologies, while you build valuable reflections, lesson plans, and activities you can use throughout your teaching career. So get ready to become an engaged learner!

Strategies for Success

Preview the contents of each section before beginning that section.
> No kidding! Take 5 minutes to scan the reflection questions and projects. It really helps!

Read the project description and reflection questions before going further.

After you preview the section, read the key articles on the CD-ROM.
> These articles have been written with you, the prospective educator, in mind.

Complete the "Key Term Definitions" in each section right after you read the article.

Locate answers to "Section Review Questions" from the corresponding article.

Explore at least three of the related articles on the Web from each section.
> Even 5 minutes at each site can reveal "nuggets" of learning you may want to revisit.

Preview the project assignment within each section before you begin the activity.

Don't attempt the reflection activities until you finish all activities in that section.

Type your reflections in a word processor and save your work as a file.
> You can then cut-and-paste your work into the reflection forms on the CD-ROM.

Keep everything!
> Your work throughout this course will serve as a resource for you to draw from in your future classroom.

Practical Recommendations

We know your life is full of competing priorities. But, don't fall behind in your assignments. Make a wall chart at the beginning of this class. Your instructor will give you all of the assignments and their due dates. Treat these like deadlines for a job. Write them on the chart. (Erasable calendars are great for this!) When you finish an assignment, erase it from the chart. Now that's immediate gratification. Reward your accomplishments. Celebrate your successes. Don't hesitate to ask your instructor for assistance. Communicate with your classmates when possible, learning should be a social activity. And most of all, remember that efforts throughout this course are an investment in the success of your future teaching career.

Technology for Teachers

- Engaged Learning
- Multimedia Student Authoring
- Software Evaluation
- Classroom Management
- Presentation Technologies
- Student Performance
- Instruction and the Internet

Introduction

A paradigm shift is taking place in American education: teachers are embracing models of instruction that are radically different from traditional educational approaches. Instructor-centered teaching methods—instructional techniques that focus on the performance of instructors: what they say and what they do—are giving way to active student-centered teaching and learning methods—instructional techniques that focus on the performance of learners: what they learn and how they learn it. Learning outcomes have become the measuring rod for quality instruction and, more and more, new media and new technologies have become the tools facilitating this change.

In the more traditional approach—the "old story"—the act of instruction is central. When instruction is the focus, the instructor is an actor on an instructional stage, and the students, as a class, are a passive audience. But with the shifting models of instruction—the "new story"—the act of learning, measured by tangible performance, is placed squarely on the shoulders of actively engaged learners. When learning is the focus, the learner is the actor and the role of the teacher changes. Instructors are not eliminated in the new models; rather instructors cease to be the only source of information and now become coaches, managers, and consultants of the multiple learning resources made available to learners. In short, instructors become guides and assistants, facilitating active student discovery and learning.

In light of this shift, the goal of the *Technology for Teachers* CD-ROM and this accompanying "portfolio workbook" is to assist "teachers-in-training" as they

- recognize and embrace the power of new media and new technologies for fulfilling the educational purpose,

- develop plans to integrate the best of the old teaching methods with all the possibilities of the new, and

- institute such plans in a controlled, coherent fashion to maximize instructional opportunities for our increasingly diverse and multicultural audience.

Technology for Teachers

In addition to these broad goals, this work also seeks to model several "best practices" for "teachers-in-training" as they

- become reflective teachers, capable of creative and critical thought about both learning theory and their own teaching strategies, and

- use authentic means of assessment, tools for measuring higher-order thinking and "real-world" skills in students.

Introduction to the *Technology for Teachers* Portfolio Workbook

As you use this workbook and the accompanying CD-ROM, you will confront new ideas and instructional strategies. It is essential that you, as a "teacher-in-training," do more than simply "**learn**" (memorize) these ideas. You must also take time to **reflect** on these ideas—to think creatively on their implications for teaching and learning—and to **apply** these ideas to concrete learning activities and strategies.

One of the preferred tools for measuring student learning and progress is the **learning portfolio**. This is the assessment model used in this workbook. As you work through these materials, you will participate in a variety of training activities designed for learning, reflecting on, and applying new information. Some of these activities will be quite conventional (i.e., multiple-choice quizzes and term identification); others will be quite innovative (i.e., online journals and interactive Web exercises). Some of the learning activities will call for individual responses, others for collaborative efforts. Whenever possible, these exercises will center on "real-world" tasks from the "everyday" experiences of teachers—lesson planning, presentation delivery, classroom management, and software evaluation—and will provide a genuinely "authentic" means of assessing your learning.

These end products of each learning activity will be placed as an "**artifact**" of learning within this portfolio workbook. Some of these materials will be entered directly into the workbook, others will involve online forms and interactive exercises that can be printed and then placed in the workbook. Taken together, all of these "artifacts" will comprise a comprehensive record of your journey through this learning experience.

We trust that this workbook and CD-ROM will provide you with a rich environment for learning and will model innovative instructional techniques you will want to make your own. We also hope that the portfolio approach of this workbook will challenge you to implement similar alternative assessment methods in your future teaching.

The Triangle of Assessment

Scholars of educational assessment argue that three levels of "evidence" are required to adequately measure student learning: (1) traditional concrete knowledge acquisition, (2) knowledge constructs and reflection, and (3) knowledge transfer and performance. Together, these three form a "triangle of evidence" of student progress.

This multidimensional approach to assessment stands in contrast to traditional "directed" learning and assessment that focus almost exclusively on factual knowledge and objective testing. The "triangle of evidence" extends assessment to higher-order thinking and the performance of "real-world" skills. This workbook addresses each side of the "triangle of evidence" when assessing learning.

A VARIETY of ARTIFACTS   LEARNING PORTFOLIO

Concrete Knowledge Acquisition

While learning is seldom limited to simple factual information (definitions, generalizations, discriminations, etc.), almost all higher-order thinking skills (problem solving, critical thinking, decision making) rest on a foundation of factual information. This "foundation knowledge" provides the "ground floor" in a learning hierarchy with each progressive level of learning building upon all lower levels. A working knowledge of calculus assumes the ability to recognize and count numbers, to add and subtract, to multiply and divide, etc. Literary criticism and creative writing both assume prior knowledge of the alphabet and basic rules of grammar.

Whenever higher-order thinking is rooted in such factual knowledge and whenever this "foundation knowledge" can be mastered through simple memorization, expect to find traditional assessment methods like "drill and practice" and multiple-choice quizzes. While such traditional means of assessment are altogether insufficient for measuring higher-level learning, they are quite sufficient for reinforcing the acquisition of concrete, factual knowledge.

To measure knowledge acquisition, this workbook includes a variety of comprehension quizzes and exercises. These materials fall into traditional categories: terminology identification, multiple-choice and true-false questions, and short answer essays. The purpose of these exercises is limited, but important: measuring student mastery of the factual, "foundation knowledge" required for teachers seeking to integrate technology tools into their instruction.

Concrete Knowledge and Information

Traditional Assessment

Technology Integration Parallel

Instructional technology can be implemented at this level. Many software titles present information at only this level, with the target objective being the memorization of terms, facts, or other information. Computerized exams, test builders, electronic encyclopedias and atlases can be implemented in this fashion. While this is of great value in the "teaching and learning cycle," educators must not limit the use of technology to only this level.

Knowledge Constructs and Reflection

Knowledge acquisition is, of course, only the first step in real learning. Beyond the rote memorization of terminology and facts, learning involves the internalization of information and the integration of new information with previously held knowledge—the analysis of new ideas, the evaluation of new information against known principles, and the synthesis of new and old thinking into a unified whole. The outcomes of higher-order thinking are thus constructed, or generated, within the mind of the learner. The process of constructing knowledge is at least as important as its final product for educators.

Of particular interest for teaching and learning is the role played by reflection, or reflective thinking, in the construction of high-order thoughts. Reflective learners compare their thoughts with those of others or against accepted principles. In reflecting on their own thoughts, these learners come to identify the principles behind their thinking, to uncover the strengths and weaknesses of their positions, to modify their thoughts, and, if necessary, to abandon failed ideas in favor of more realistic and functional ones.

To measure the construction of higher-order thinking, this workbook includes both structured and open-ended reflection journal exercises as well as collaborative "discussions" that elicit interaction between learners. All of these activities are designed to encourage "reflective," self-critical thinking and the internalization of new ideas into the learner's thoughts.

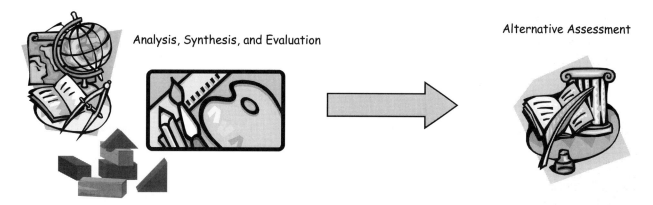

Analysis, Synthesis, and Evaluation

Alternative Assessment

Technology Integration Parallel

Here again, we find technology implemented in classrooms with activities involving higher-order thinking skills. Software designed to connect to preconstructed knowledge, encourage analysis and reflection through role playing and simulations, and empower students with the ability to create their own reflections in the form of electronic journals is becoming more common. Educators quickly see an increase in motivation as their students are encouraged to take active roles with the technology by reflecting and expressing their new knowledge.

Knowledge Transfer and Performance

The exclusive use of traditional testing—especially multiple-choice examinations—continues to draw widespread criticism. This type of testing frequently measures only lower-order thinking skills while ignoring essential higher-order thinking altogether. To remedy this situation, many educators are turning to performance-based assessment, an emerging form of assessment that requires a learner to demonstrate the behavior to be measured. If writing skills are to be measured, the student is required to write an essay. Foreign language students are required to converse with their instructors in a foreign language.

Authentic assessment takes performance-based assessment one step further. With authentic assessment, the behavior to be measured must be a "real-world" skill. To measure writing skills, a student writes a business letter. The economics student is required to develop a business plan. Mathematics students are required to balance checkbooks. This "real-world" assessment demands that learners apply knowledge and skills rather than simply remember the facts of a given academic subject. Even further, the assessment does not occur as an isolated act, but is embedded into the act of instruction. Planning authentic assessment is the first stage in designing a teaching and learning unit to be delivered in a classroom.

To measure the application of learning to "real-world" situations, this workbook includes a variety of simulated and "real-world" activities ranging from software and Web site evaluations and lesson plan construction to Web page development and classroom interviews. In each case, these exercises are designed to ensure the successful transfer of knowledge to "real-life" instructional tasks.

Transfer, Application, and Performance

Authentic Assessment

The performance is the assessment!

Technology Integration Parallel

Computer technology is an excellent tool for authentic assessment. Simulation software allows students to perform otherwise impossible tasks. Virtual field trips and "expert forums" open up new worlds to isolated students and classrooms through Internet technologies. Multimedia authoring software and presentation technologies allow students to create and apply new knowledge, and, through Internet publishing, to share their personal knowledge and creations with the world. As educational systems continue to embrace these technologies, students will be better prepared to lead productive, rewarding lives, and to take active, constructive roles in our society.

Promoting Engaged Learning

Instructional technology must be a catalyst of real educational reform. Technology tools, if correctly utilized, can speed the shift from teacher-centered to student-centered learning. Under the guiding hand of a creative teacher, technology tools can engage active learners in their own learning process—learning becomes a matter of discovery, reflection, and collaboration. "Technology for technology's sake"—the false notion that the purchase of technology tools will automatically result in educational change—is naïve and even dangerous. Today's teachers must themselves be learners and leaders if technology is to be successfully embraced and integrated into instruction.

To introduce "Promoting Engaged Learning," the *Technology for Teachers* CD-ROM includes the following materials:

"The Old Story and New Story: Shifting Models in Teaching and Learning" challenges educators to embrace the paradigm shift from teacher-centered to student-centered, activity-based learning.

"The Evolving Classroom: Enabling, Enhancing, Extending, and Engaging Learning" provides a general description of the evolving classroom as educators explore enabling, enhancing, extending, and engaging learners in rich learning environments.

"Learning Styles: Targeting Instruction to Learner's Needs" investigates the different ways individuals process information, characteristics often referred to as "learning styles."

"Basic Computing Concepts: A Brief Introduction for Educators" explores the world of microcomputers and introduces basic computer-related terminology in an easy-to-read narrative.

To access these materials, load the CD-ROM, select the "Promoting Engaged Learning" icon, and click the desired article title.

In addition, this portfolio workbook contains the following learning activities:

Review Questions: Promoting Engaged Learning
15 Terms Every Teacher Should Know
Key Article Quiz: Basic Computing Concepts
Online Activity: Reviewing Engaged Learning Web Sites
Structured Reflection Journal
Open Reflection Journal

Promoting Engaged Learning

To motivate today's learner, teachers must excel at more than subject matter. We must harness the power of creativity and knowledge within each and every student. We educators can no longer view learners as passive recipients of information, we must now see students as active participants who take ownership of the learning process.

SECTIONS:

* **Shifting Models in Teaching and Learning**
* **The Evolving Classroom**
* **Learning Styles**
* **Basic Computing Concepts**

Section Review Questions

1) Recognizing that learning occurs outside the regular school day is a primary attribute of which stage in the evolving classroom?
   a) enabled learning environments   b) enhanced learning environments
   c) extended learning environments d) enlightened learning environments

2) Which of the following is considered a weakness or barrier of engaged learning environments?
   a) promotes student ownership   b) connects to real world
   c) very time-consuming   d) provides meaningful collaboration

3) When an instructor models the use of presentation technology in a traditional lecture, which stage of technology integration are they exhibiting?
   a) engaged learning   b) enhanced learning   c) extended learning   d) enabled learning

4) Instructor-centered teaching methods are giving way to active _____-_____ teaching and learning methods.

5) When the focus of education is on the instructor and the act of instruction, curriculum goals are established to guide performance of _____ _____.

6) When the focus is placed on actively engaging students' minds, the goals shift to measurable statements of _____ _____.

7) Characteristic strengths and preferences in the way individuals process information are called _____ _____.

8) What do the initials L.S.I. stand for? _____ _____
   _____

9) "Musical" is one of the multiple intelligences recognized by Howard Gardner.   TRUE   FALSE

10) The brain of the computer is the "microprocessor," or CPU chip.   TRUE   FALSE

15 Terms Nobody Wants to Memorize, but Every Teacher Should Know

1) assessment:

_____

_____

2) engaged learning:

_____

3) auditory learner:

_____

4) learning styles:

_____

5) LSI :

_____

6) hardware:

_____

7) software applications:

_____

8) RAM:

_____

9) megabyte:

_____

10) function keys:

_____

11) ports:

_____

12) modem:

_____

13) operating system:

_____

14) directory:

_____

15) spreadsheet:

_____

_____

These questions are drawn from the "**Basic Computing Concepts: A Brief Introduction for Educators**" article on the CD-ROM.

1. A mouse may be used for all of the following EXCEPT . . .

    A. moving the cursor in a word processor.
    B. operating a graphical user interface (GUI) such as Microsoft Windows 95/98.
    C. selecting items from menus or lists.
    D. transferring data from one computer to another.

2. A collection of related pieces of information that is stored as a single unit on a floppy or hard disk is referred to as . . .

    A. an operating system.
    B. a file.
    C. a spreadsheet.
    D. a record.

3. To format a disk means to . . .

    A. copy its entire contents to another disk.
    B. delete specified files from it.
    C. prepare or initialize it for use.
    D. load a software program.

4. Which software application is best for producing term papers?

    A. a word processor
    B. an electronic spreadsheet
    C. a desktop publisher
    D. a database manager

5. A communication device that connects one computer to another or to an information system via telephone lines is called . . .

    A. a laser printer.
    B. a scanner.
    C. the central processing unit (CPU).
    D. a modem.

6. A library's card catalog is a good example of . . .

    A. a spreadsheet.
    B. desktop publishing.
    C. a database.
    D. project management.

7. Computer files are permanently stored . . .

    A. in Random Access Memory (RAM).
    B. on disks (hard or floppy).
    C. by printers.
    D. by keyboards.

8. You can move the cursor through a word processing document with . . .

    A. the NUM LOCK key.
    B. the arrow keys.
    C. the alphabet keys.
    D. the function keys.

9. In an address book database, the entry for "Phone Number" would best be described as . . .

    A. a record.
    B. a file.
    C. a database.
    D. a field.

10. Which of the following is NOT a primary function of an electronic spreadsheet?

    A. storing numerical records
    B. publishing long text documents
    C. performing calculations
    D. performing mathematical analysis

11. The "heart" of the computer (where all the processing of information occurs) is the . . .

    A. microprocessor (the CPU chip).
    B. disk drive.
    C. video overlay card.
    D. modem.

12. The application in which you would most likely find text formatting features like line centering, underlining, italicizing, and page numbering is . . .

    A. a database manager.
    B. a project manager.
    C. a programming language.
    D. a word processor.

13. The function of a label in a spreadsheet is to . . .

    A. provide raw data (numbers) for calculation.
    B. present the results of calculations.
    C. describe the numerical data stored in the corresponding row or column.
    D. present financial analysis.

14. Which is the largest unit of memory?

    A. a byte
    B. a megabyte
    C. a kilobyte
    D. Random Access Memory

15. Computer peripherals (like printers and scanners) are connected to the central processing unit by cables attached to . . .

    A. a modem.
    B. a mouse.
    C. an expansion card.
    D. a port.

16. A software package that oversees the communication and translation of commands between hardware and application programs is called . . .

    A. an operating system.
    B. a mainframe computer.
    C. a Web browser.
    D. a graphical user interface.

17. The structured storage and retrieval of non-numerical data is best achieved with an . . .

    A. CAD/CAM program.
    B. electronic spreadsheet.
    C. word processor.
    D. database manager.

18. Which application would best organize a long mailing list of names, addresses, cities, states, and zip codes?

    A. a word processor
    B. a database manager
    C. an electronic spreadsheet
    D. an operating system

19. The point at which text is entered into a word processing document is called . . .

    A. the cursor.
    B. the INSERT mode.
    C. a menu.
    D. a speed button.

20. If you wish to computerize your household budget, you should use . . .

    A. an electronic spreadsheet.
    B. a database manager.
    C. a graphics program.
    D. a word processor.

21. Which statement is true about a computer file?

    A. There is no limitation to the size of a file.
    B. An unlimited number of files can be stored on a disk.
    C. Any number and combination of characters may be used in a filename.
    D. Two files with the same name cannot exist in the same directory on the same disk.

22. In a database, all information associated with a unique person, transaction, or entry is called a . . .

    A. file.
    B. field.
    C. record.
    D. database.

23. Which of the following is NOT an advantage of hard disk storage?

    A. Hard disks have more storage capacity than floppies.
    B. All hard disks are portable and transportable.
    C. Hard disks access information faster than floppies.
    D. A program on a hard disk runs faster than one on a floppy.

24. Which of the following is true regarding RAM?

    A. RAM measures the storage capacity of a hard disk.
    B. Information in RAM is lost when the computer is turned off.
    C. RAM is measured as high density and low density.
    D. All programs require the same amount of RAM.

25. The automatic movement of a word that does not fit at the end of one line to the beginning of the next line is called . . .

    A. right justification.
    B. a "hard" return.
    C. word wrap.
    D. automatic indention.

26. Saving data frequently prevents . . .

    A. the necessity of re-entering data.
    B. the loss of files on a hard disk.
    C. the loss of temporary files created during editing.
    D. software and hardware crashes.

27. Which of the following is NOT an example of hardware?

    A. a monitor
    B. a keyboard
    C. a database manager
    D. a printer

28. How many kilobytes equal one megabyte?

    A. 10
    B. 100
    C. 1000
    D. 1,000,000

Reviewing Engaged Learning Web Sites

ACTIVITY INSTRUCTIONS

STEP ONE:
Launch your Web browser. Insert the *Technology for Teachers* CD-ROM. Open the "index.htm" file on the CD. Click the "Promoting Engaged Learning" icon.

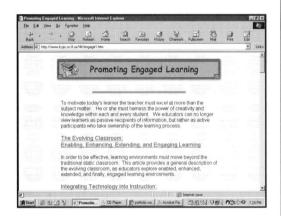

Let's take some time to look at other materials available on the Internet regarding *engaged learning*. On the companion CD-ROM, you will find a variety of links to World Wide Web sites containing a wealth of supportive information. In this exercise, you will be asked to review one of these Web sites and share the information with at least one of your classmates. Follow the instructions printed on this page to access these sites. You will need "live access" to the Internet.

1) Pick a Partner in your Class (this is an example of "cooperative learning").
2) Select a Web Site to Review.
3) Review your Web Site and Record your Comments on the Form on the Next Page.
4) Discuss and Present your Web Site to your Partner.
5) Record Observations about your Partner's Site.

STEP TWO:
Scroll down this page until you see "Online Resources."

This section of the page contains links to related Web sites. To access a site, simply slide your mouse over the desired link and click. Your browser will leave the contents of the CD-ROM and load the appropriate Web page. The Internet is a very dynamic environment. Several Web sites may have moved since the publication of the CD-ROM. If you receive an error message, make sure your connection to the Internet is functioning (check a popular Web site). Try other links to related sites as necessary.

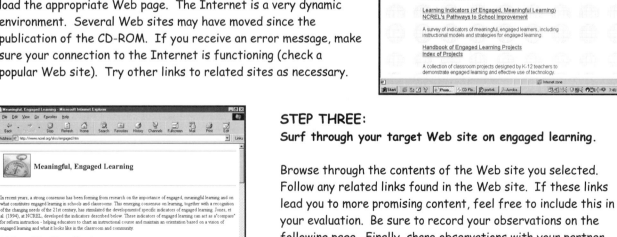

STEP THREE:
Surf through your target Web site on engaged learning.

Browse through the contents of the Web site you selected. Follow any related links found in the Web site. If these links lead you to more promising content, feel free to include this in your evaluation. Be sure to record your observations on the following page. Finally, share observations with your partner and record your partner's comments.

Your Engaged Learning Web Site Review

List the URL: http:// _____

Title of Web Site: _____

Describe the main idea or message of the site.

_____

_____

What was the most valuable insight to engaged learning, learning styles, or learning theory that you found at this site?

_____

_____

_____

How could you apply the information at this site to assist you in teaching?

_____

_____

_____

Your Partner's Engaged Learning Web Site Review

List the URL: http://_____

Title of Web Site: _____

Describe the main idea or message of the site.

_____

_____

What was the most valuable insight to engaged learning, learning styles, or learning theory that you found at this site?

_____

_____

_____

How could you apply the information at this site to assist you in teaching?

_____

_____

_____

Structured Reflection Journal

Write several paragraphs on your thoughts and opinions regarding "Engaged Learning." Check with your instructor for the desired length of your response. Consider responding to:

- Is engaged learning a valid objective for schools and other educational institutions? Why?

- What benefits would engaged learning have for the work force and business community?

- Why are learning styles important in the design of instruction?

- Why is Gardner's theory of multiple intelligences so popular among educators?

- Why is understanding basic computing concepts essential for all educators?

JOURNAL INSTRUCTIONS

STEP ONE:
1) Insert the *Technology for Teachers* CD-ROM.
2) If the CD-ROM does not auto-load, launch your Web browser and open the "index.htm" file on the CD-ROM. This file can be found in the ROOT folder of the CD-ROM. (That's the first folder that opens when you double click on the icon to look at your CD-ROM drive contents.) This page will load in your browser.
3) Click the "Promoting Engaged Learning" icon.
4) Scroll to the "Interactive Exercises" section of this page and click the desired question under "Structured Journal Exercises."

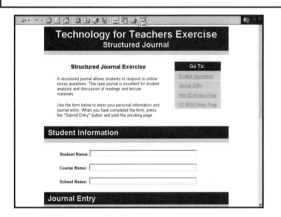

STEP TWO:
Click in each field of the "Structured Journal" form and enter the following:

1) Type your name (first name, then last).
2) Type the name of this course.
3) Type the name of your school or college.
4) Type your journal entry in the "Comments" field. Entries can be up to 20 pages of text in length and can be copied and pasted to the form from a word processor. Remember to place a "double-spaced" return between paragraphs.

STEP THREE: Submit Entry

Click the button located at the bottom of the form. This will produce a Web page in your browser with your comments. Click the "Print" button in your browser. This will print your journal entry.

Place this journal entry inside the portfolio workbook to complete the assignment. Your instructor will give you due dates for each activity.

Promoting Engaged Learning

Open Reflection Journal

Questions for Reflection Journals

The purpose of the "open reflection" exercise is to encourage you to document your insights and questions about this topic. This record of your thoughts can serve as a "springboard" for reflective thinking – the beginning of an "internal dialogue" with your own thoughts as you gain more knowledge and experience. While this exercise is truly open-ended (that is, you can enter any comment you desire), consider writing about broad questions like the following:

- What is the most important lesson you have learned in this section? Why?
- What are your personal strengths and weaknesses in this area?
- How would you implement what you have learned about this topic in a classroom? What specific strategies would you use? What type of lesson plans would you develop?
- What is the greatest obstacle for using this type of technology in traditional classrooms?
- What questions remain unanswered about this topic?

JOURNAL INSTRUCTIONS
STEP ONE:
From the CD-ROM home page, select the "Promoting Engaged Learning" icon. Next, scroll down to the "Interactive Web Exercises" section and click the "Reflection Journal" option.

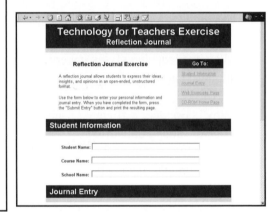

STEP TWO:

Click in each field on the form that appears, and type the following;

Type in your name and the name of your course and school. In the "Entry Title" field, type a meaningful title for your entry. Click in the comment field directly below and begin typing your journal entry. Remember, you can write your reflection in a word processing program, run spelling and grammar checking, and "cut-and-paste" your work into the comment field.

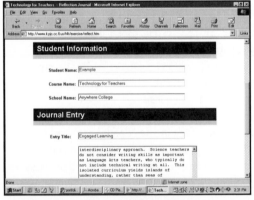

STEP THREE: Submit Entry

Click the button located at the bottom of the form. This will produce a Web page in your browser with your comments. Click the "Print" button in your browser. This will print your journal entry.

Place this journal entry inside the portfolio workbook to complete the assignment. Your instructor will give you due dates for each activity.

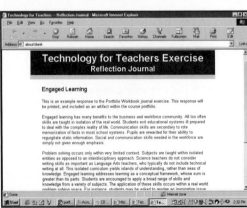

Multimedia Student Authoring

Multimedia student authoring moves the traditional practice of student-created reports to an exciting new level. Instructors provide students with rich environments of resource materials—traditional research documents (books and pamphlets), audio and video tapes, collections of images, computer software and multimedia encyclopedias, etc.—as well as highly structured, easy-to-use authoring software, like the very popular HyperStudio or Digital Chisel programs. From these resources, students "construct" multimedia reports and portfolios, excellent tools for assessing critical thinking and higher-order learning.

To introduce "Multimedia Student Authoring," the *Technology for Teachers* CD-ROM includes the following materials:

"The Elements of Multimedia: Traditional Media on Computers" surveys the various multimedia elements—sound, graphics, animation, and video—used in educational software and interactive classrooms.

"Harvesting the Web: Obtaining Text, Graphics, and Multimedia from the Web" provides a simple set of guidelines for downloading text and graphics from Web sites.

"Multimedia Student Authoring: Authentic Assessment and Electronic Portfolios" introduces student-built multimedia projects and the possibilities of electronic portfolios for assessing learning.

To access these materials, load the CD-ROM, select the "Multimedia Student Authoring" icon, and click the desired article title.

In addition, this portfolio workbook contains the following learning activities:

Review Questions: Multimedia Student Authoring
15 Terms Every Teacher Should Know
Online Activity: Multimedia Scavenger Hunt
"Hands-On" Activity: Building Multimedia Reports
Structured Reflection Journal
Open Reflection Journal

Multimedia Student Authoring

When measuring student progress moves beyond traditional testing to portfolio assessment, teachers begin to build more accurate records of the student learning experience. Student authoring and multimedia portfolios are especially powerful tools for more authentic assessment.

SECTIONS:

* The Elements of Multimedia
* Harvesting the Web
* Multimedia Student Authoring

Section Review Questions

1) Which of the following is NOT currently considered an element of electronic multimedia?
    a) text   b) sound
    c) taste   d) video

2) What types of images are made up of dots, like images in a newspaper?
    a) vector images   b) raster images
    c) linear images   d) fractal images

3) Which of the following is NOT a type of digital video format?
    a) AVI   b) M-PEG   c) Quicktime   d) LRC

4) When discussing the Internet and World Wide Web, the maximum capacity speed at which files are transmitted is called . . .
    a) linear limit.   b) bandwidth.   c) digital capacity.   d) horizon limit.

5) When harvesting media from the Web, follow the rules of _____ _____, gathering files for educational use only.

6) To copy an image from a Web site, _____ -click on the image in your Web browser.

7) Student _____ _____ tools are designed to empower the learner with the ability to manipulate multimedia.

8) It is no longer sufficient to measure student performance through a battery of
_____ _____ _____.

9) Portfolios generally become more valuable when they include multimedia components.
    TRUE   FALSE

10) When individuals act as users of knowledge, rather than just recipients of information, motivation and retention increases.
    TRUE   FALSE

15 Terms Nobody Wants to Memorize, but Every Teacher Should Know

1) multimedia:

_____

_____

2) multimedia literacy:

_____

_____

3) animation:

_____

_____

4) file compression:

_____

_____

5) streaming media:

_____

_____

6) video capture cards:

_____

_____

7) OCR software:

_____

_____

8) video frame grabbers:

_____

_____

9) slide/photo scanners:

_____

_____

10) clip-art collections:

_____

11) HyperStudio:

_____

12) Digital Chisel:

_____

Use the Web to define the following:
13) "fair use":

_____

_____

14) copyright:

_____

_____

15) trademark:

_____

Multimedia Scavenger Hunt

In this exercise, you will go on a multimedia scavenger hunt. Load the *Technology for Teachers* CD-ROM and select the "Interactive Exercises" icon. Choose the "Web Search Tools" option to load a list of popular Web search engines. Use these tools to locate the following items. Save each of the items to a 3.5" floppy diskette or print them from your Web browser. Include these "artifacts" in your portfolio workbook. Have fun and good luck!

	Checkbox	Item	Web Location (URL)
1		Photo of Abraham Lincoln	http://
2		Map of Antarctica	
3		Photo of Stephen Hawking	
4		Image of a chemical molecule	
5		Photo of Mount Everest	
6		Sound file of a train	
7		Painting by van Gogh	
8		Voice clip of John F. Kennedy	
9		Top story photo from CNN	
10		Any animated GIF	
11		An animated GIF of planet Earth	
12		A map of Eritrea	
13		Any song (don't save to diskette)	
14		Any historical video clip (don't save to diskette)	
15		A photo of your favorite actor or actress	
16		A photo from your favorite state in the U.S.	
17		A photo of Michelangelo's *Pieta*	
18		A photo of your favorite athlete	
19		The logo of the next Summer Olympics	
20		A weather map for today's weather in Atlanta, Georgia	

Multimedia Student Authoring

Building Multimedia Reports

This exercise allows the student to plan a multimedia authoring project using storyboards. (See the next page for guidelines for building successful storyboards.) Students will combine the results of their research and various forms of media (text, graphics, sounds, digital movies, etc.) to create a "visual outline" of their report.

If possible, we encourage students to convert their storyboards into computerized reports using one of the simple authoring tools like HyperStudio or Digital Chisel. If these software packages are not available, a presentation tool—like Microsoft PowerPoint—can be used to build multimedia authoring projects. The results of this exercise, whether "paper" or storyboards or computer files saved to disk, should be saved as artifacts in the portfolio workbook.

The following pages provide you with templates to create a storyboard for your work. Complete the storyboard using the guidelines on this page.

STEP ONE: Select the topic. Create a project to share with other students. The topic can focus on the subject matter, or grade level, you would like to teach or are currently teaching. Check with your instructor for approval of the topic before beginning work.

STEP TWO: Complete a storyboard on paper using the templates on the following pages in this workbook. Copy additional pages as needed. An effective report/presentation will follow this pattern:

> Title Page
> List of Topics (menu, outline)
> Content Pages (containing subject matter)
> Closing Page (summary of ideas)

STEP THREE: Gather the media for your presentation. The availability of digital media capture devices will determine how you gather media. Start with scanners and "harvesting the Web." (See the article on "Harvesting the Web" for guidelines on gathering media.) Add audio and video if the appropriate capture devices are available.

STEP FOUR: Use multimedia authoring software to create your report or presentation. Use HyperStudio or Digital Chisel if available. Microsoft PowerPoint or other presentation software can also be used to build multimedia projects. Check with your instructor for availability and further instructions.

STEP FIVE: Include this work in the portfolio workbook.

What Are Storyboards?

Planning a report or multimedia presentation can be a challenging proposition. Before you begin a project, it's a good idea to create an outline or "script" of the items you will cover, the order in which you will cover them, and the overall graphical layout of your work. This outline is often referred to as a storyboard. A storyboard is a graphical representation—a visual outline—of a complete multimedia project. Think of it as a blueprint for successful media projects. Here are a few guidelines to follow.

Guidelines:

- The storyboard should be neat and easily read.
- The storyboard should represent an entire project, with an introduction, body, and conclusion.
- Each element to be included on every slide should be noted in the storyboard, including
  - titles and headings
  - text
  - graphics
  - navigation buttons and objects
  - names of digital media files to be included
- Graphic images should be placed on a "stage" within the storyboard template.
- Media file names should be listed on the slide or page where they will be placed.
- Media files can include sound, music, animation, and video files.
- Navigation buttons and objects should be clearly visible.
- Arrows should be drawn, clearly indicating links between slides/pages.

Taking the time to create a storyboard of any project saves a lot of time and frustration later. In classrooms with limited computer resources, storyboards are an absolute must. Students must know what slides or pages they are going to create, what text they will enter, and what media they have access to in their project. Storyboarding optimizes the productivity of students using computers. Some students build their projects on computers, while others plan their projects at media workstations. (See the "Classroom Management and Facilities Design" article on the CD-ROM for a full discussion of the "workstation rotation" model for building multimedia projects.) This workbook contains storyboard templates for planning multimedia projects. Be sure to check the materials in the appendix or in the "Interactive Web Exercises" section of the CD-ROM for more of these templates for future use. Below are examples of icons found in many storyboards.

Sound Icon	Help Icon		Previous Page	Menu/Home	Next Page

Multimedia Storyboard

Student Name: _____ Course # _____ Section #_____

TITLE SLIDE/PAGE

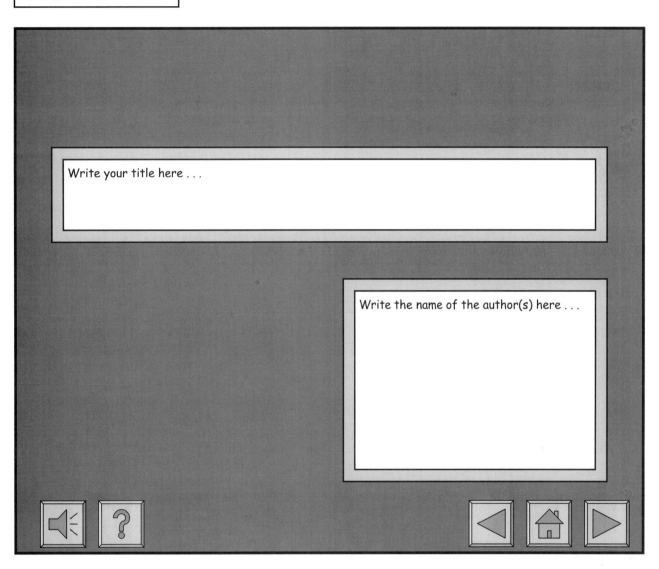

Write your title here . . .

Write the name of the author(s) here . . .

Media List: List each media item you would include on this slide/page.

Images: filenames _____ , _____

Sounds: filenames _____ , _____

Video/Animation/Other: _____ , _____

Multimedia Storyboard

MENU SLIDE/PAGE

Write your slide/page title here . . .

Write your topic titles here . . . (you might use the titles of your subsequent pages)

Media List: List each media item you would include on this slide/page.

Images: filenames _____ , _____

Sounds: filenames _____ , _____

Video/Animation/Other: _____ , _____

Multimedia Storyboard

CONTENT SLIDE/PAGE

Write your slide/page title here . . .

Media Stage:

Use this area to place graphics.

You can even use printed images. Simply "cut-and-paste" pictures you wish to use on this page here.

Scissors and Glue :)

Media Caption:
_____
_____
_____

Write your slide/page content here . . .
_____
_____
_____
_____
_____
_____
_____
_____
_____
_____
_____
_____
_____
_____
_____
_____

Media List: List each media item you would include on this slide/page.

Images: filenames _____ , _____

Sounds: filenames _____ , _____

Video/Animation/Other: _____ , _____

Multimedia Storyboard

CONTENT SLIDE/PAGE

Write your slide/page title here . . .

Write your slide/page content here . . .

_____
_____
_____
_____
_____
_____
_____
_____
_____
_____
_____
_____

Media Stage:

Use this area to place graphics.

You can even use printed images. Simply "cut-and-paste" pictures you wish to use on this page here.

Scissors and Glue :)

Media Caption:
_____
_____

Media List: List each media item you would include on this slide/page.

Images: filenames _____ , _____

Sounds: filenames _____ , _____

Video/Animation/Other: _____ , _____

Multimedia Storyboard

CONTENT SLIDE/PAGE

Write your slide/page title here . . .

Media Stage:

Use this area to place graphics.

You can even use printed images. Simply "cut-and-paste" pictures you wish to use on this page here.

Scissors and Glue :)

Write your slide/page content here . . .

_____

_____

_____

_____

_____

_____

_____

_____

_____

_____

_____

_____

_____

_____

_____

Media Caption:
_____
_____
_____

Media List: List each media item you would include on this slide/page.

Images: filenames _____ , _____

Sounds: filenames _____ , _____

Video/Animation/Other: _____ , _____

Multimedia Storyboard

CONTENT SLIDE/PAGE

Write your slide/page title here . . .

Write your slide/page content here . . .

_____
_____
_____
_____
_____
_____
_____
_____
_____
_____
_____
_____
_____
_____

Media Stage:

Use this area to place graphics.

You can even use printed images. Simply "cut-and-paste" pictures you wish to use on this page here.

Scissors and Glue :)

Media Caption:
_____
_____
_____

Media List: List each media item you would include on this slide/page.

Images: filenames _____ , _____

Sounds: filenames _____ , _____

Video/Animation/Other: _____ , _____

Multimedia Storyboard

CONTENT SLIDE/PAGE

Write your slide/page title here . . .

Media Stage:

Use this area to place graphics.

You can even use printed images. Simply "cut-and-paste" pictures you wish to use on this page here.

Scissors and Glue :)

Media Caption:
_____
_____
_____

Write your slide/page content here . . .
_____
_____
_____
_____
_____
_____
_____
_____
_____
_____
_____
_____
_____

Media List: List each media item you would include on this slide/page.

Images: filenames _____ , _____

Sounds: filenames _____ , _____

Video/Animation/Other: _____ , _____

Multimedia Storyboard

CONTENT SLIDE/PAGE

Write your slide/page title here . . .

Write your slide/page content here . . .

_____
_____
_____
_____
_____
_____
_____
_____
_____
_____
_____
_____
_____

Media Stage:

Use this area to place graphics.

You can even use printed images. Simply "cut-and-paste" pictures you wish to use on this page here.

Scissors and Glue :)

Media Caption:
_____
_____
_____

Media List: List each media item you would include on this slide/page.

Images: filenames _____ , _____

Sounds: filenames _____ , _____

Video/Animation/Other: _____ , _____

Multimedia Storyboard

CONCLUSION SLIDE/PAGE

Write your slide/page title here . . .

Write closing thoughts here . . .

Media List: List each media item you would include on this slide/page.

Images: filenames _____ , _____

Sounds: filenames _____ , _____

Video/Animation/Other: _____ , _____

Multimedia Student Authoring

Structured Reflection Journal

Write several paragraphs on your thoughts and opinions regarding "Multimedia Student Authoring." Check with your instructor for the desired length of your response. Consider responding to:

- What are the benefits of student-created multimedia projects?

- How might a unit of instruction based on multimedia student authoring be delivered in a classroom?

- Describe HyperStudio and/or Digital Chisel. Why do you think these programs are so popular?

- The price of digitizing equipment, such as scanners and video capture cards, is dropping rapidly. How might this affect an average classroom? What advantages might this offer students and parents?

JOURNAL INSTRUCTIONS

STEP ONE:
1) Insert the *Technology for Teachers* CD-ROM.
2) If the CD-ROM does not auto-load, launch your Web browser and open the "index.htm" file on the CD-ROM. This file can be found in the ROOT folder of the CD-ROM. (That's the first folder that opens when you double click on the icon to look at your CD-ROM drive contents.) This page will load in your browser.
3) Click the "Multimedia Student Authoring" icon.
4) Scroll to the "Interactive Exercises" section of this page and click the desired question under "Structured Journal Exercises."

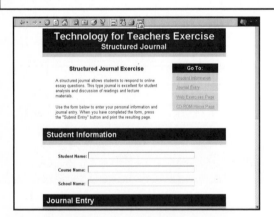

STEP TWO:
Click in each field of the "Structured Journal" form and enter the following:

1) Type your name (first name, then last).
2) Type the name of this course.
3) Type the name of your school or college.
4) Type your journal entry in the "Comments" field. Entries can be up to 20 pages of text in length and can be copied and pasted to the form from a word processor. Remember to place a "double-spaced" return between paragraphs.

STEP THREE:

Submit Entry

Click the button located at the bottom of the form. This will produce a Web page in your browser with your comments. Click the "Print" button in your browser. This will print your journal entry.

Place this journal entry inside the portfolio workbook to complete the assignment. Your instructor will give you due dates for each activity.

Open Reflection Journal

Questions for Reflection Journals

The purpose of the "open reflection" exercise is to encourage you to document your insights and questions about this topic. This record of your thoughts can serve as a "springboard" for reflective thinking—the beginning of an "internal dialogue" with your own thoughts as you gain more knowledge and experience. While this exercise is truly open-ended (that is, you can enter any comment you desire), consider writing about broad questions like the following:

- What is the most important lesson you have learned in this section? Why?
- What are your personal strengths and weaknesses in this area?
- How would you implement what you have learned about this topic in a classroom? What specific strategies would you use? What type of lesson plans would you develop?
- What is the greatest obstacle for using this type of technology in traditional classrooms?
- What questions remain unanswered about this topic?

JOURNAL INSTRUCTIONS
STEP ONE:
From the CD-ROM home page, select the "Multimedia Student Authoring" icon. Next, scroll down to the "Interactive Web Exercises" section and click the "Reflection Journal" option.

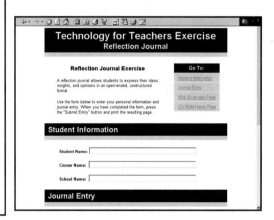

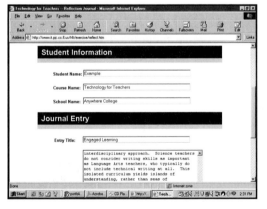

STEP TWO:

Click in each field on the form that appears, and type the following:

Type in your name and the name of your course and school. In the "Entry Title" field, type a meaningful title for your entry. Click in the comment field directly below and begin typing your journal entry. Remember, you can write your reflection in a word processing program, run spelling and grammar checking, and "cut-and-paste" your work into the comment field.

STEP THREE:

Click the button located at the bottom of the form. This will produce a Web page in your browser with your comments. Click the "Print" button in your browser. This will print your journal entry.

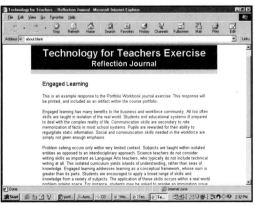

Place this journal entry inside the portfolio workbook to complete the assignment. Your instructor will give you due dates for each activity.

Evaluating Instructional Software

Software evaluation skills are essential for the active instructor. Limited budgets and the overwhelming number of educational software titles demand a structured approach to assessing the value of these tools for communicating and reinforcing learning. With the advent of the multimedia CD-ROM and now with the blossoming of interactive Web sites, the possibilities for technology-enhanced learning have never been greater. But instructors must choose wisely among these tools. Clear evaluation guidelines must direct instructors as they seek to integrate educational software into the learning environment.

To introduce "Evaluating Instructional Software," the *Technology for Teachers* CD-ROM includes the following materials:

"Building Blocks of Computer-Assisted Instruction: Tutorials, Drill and Practice, Games, and Simulations" investigates the strengths and weaknesses of the four major modes of computer-assisted instruction.

"Evaluating Educational Software: A Structured Approach" provides a checklist of questions for ranking the effectiveness of educational software.

"Evaluating Educational Web Sites: A Structured Approach" offers criteria for evaluating the educational potential of Web-based materials.

To access these materials, load the CD-ROM, select the "Evaluating Educational Software" icon, and click the desired article title.

In addition, this portfolio workbook contains the following learning activities:

Review Questions: Evaluating Educational Software
15 Terms Every Teacher Should Know
Key Article Quiz: "Building Blocks of Computer-Assisted Instruction"
Online Activity: "Jigsaw" Team Collaboration
Online Activity: Educational Software Evaluation
Structured Reflection Journal
Open Reflection Journal

Evaluating Instructional Software

The explosion of the educational software market is providing instructors with new and exciting teaching tools. But the overwhelming number of software titles—and their varying quality—requires instructors to carefully evaluate these tools before purchase. Structured guidelines for measuring the educational effectiveness of software and Web resources are essential.

SECTIONS:

* Building Blocks of Computer-Assisted Instruction
* Evaluating Educational Software
* Evaluating Educational Web Sites

Section Review Questions

1) Which of the following is NOT considered a category of instructional software?
    a) drill and practice software   b) simulation software
    c) tutorials   d) emulation software

2) Drill and practice is NOT an effective tool for . . .
    a) teaching basic skills   b) motivating learners
    c) reinforcing previous training   d) offering initial training

3) In which type of exercise is the learner required to bring together several different sets of previously held knowledge or skills to deduce a correct answer?
    a) transfer of information   b) discrimination   c) generalization   d) reinforcement

4) In which type of exercise is the learner required to evaluate a list of items in light of criteria established by a question?
    a) transfer of information   b) discrimination   c) generalization   d) reinforcement

5) Recall questions require the learner to provide a response to a question without any prompts or _____ _____.

6) "True-false" and multiple-choice questions fit the _____ mold .

7) Computer tutorials are training tools in which new information is taught, verified, and reinforced through _____ with a computer.

8) Tutorials are especially useful when _____ amounts of information must be taught.

9) With educational software, content is king.

   TRUE   FALSE

10) The missing ingredient in most education Web sites is interaction.

   TRUE   FALSE

15 Terms Nobody Wants to Memorize, but Every Teacher Should Know

1) simulations:
_____
_____

2) recall questions:
_____

3) recognition questions:
_____

4) tutorial narratives:
_____

5) conditional branching:
_____

6) decision points/paths:
_____

7) learner level:
_____

8) system requirements:
_____
_____

Use the Web to define the following:
9) user interface:
_____

10) navigation buttons:
_____

11) license agreement:
_____

12) software piracy:
_____

13) online journal:
_____

14) browser:
_____

15) search engine:
_____

These questions are drawn from the "**Building Blocks of Computer-Assisted Instruction: Tutorials, Drill and Practice, Games, and Simulations**" article on the CD-ROM.

1) Drill and practice is designed to teach new information or skills; that is, drill and practice is not designed to reinforce previous training, knowledge, or skills. TRUE FALSE

2) Which of the following CAI tools is best for teaching higher-order thinking skills (decision making and problem solving)?
      A. drill and practice   B. educational games
      C. tutorials   D. simulations

Matching: Match the statements below with the appropriate term: generalization, discrimination, or synthesis. Write the term in the space provided.

3) A student knows that all mammals have hair, recognizes that a certain animal is a mammal, and concludes that this animal must have hair. _____

4) A student is presented with this list—dogs, cats, monkeys, horses—and is expected to recognize that all of these are mammals. _____

5) A student is presented with this list—dogs, cats, crocodiles, horses—and is expected to identify the non-mammal. _____

6) Recall questions require the learner to provide a response to a question without any prompts or optional choices; while recognition questions provide the learner with a list of alternative responses from which to choose. TRUE FALSE

7) Identify the following question types as recall or recognition questions. Write the appropriate word—recall or recognition—in the blank.

_____ True-False
_____ Multiple Choice
_____ Matching
_____ Fill-in-the-Blank
_____ Essay

8) Since grading recall questions requires sophisticated answer judging, easier-to-grade recognition questions are better for computer-assisted instruction. TRUE FALSE

9) Which of the following is the most important element in successful drill and practice?

A. high quality feedback to student responses B. use of recall rather than recognition questions
C. variety of question and answer formats   D. early exit options to prevent student frustration

10) Which CAI tool is best for introducing learners to large amounts of factual information?

      A. drill and practice
      B. tutorials
      C. educational games
      D. simulations

11) Tutorials are often designed to replace traditional textbook or lecture presentations of training materials. TRUE FALSE

12) While computer tutorials are excellent tools for teaching factual materials, they are less effective for teaching complex processes or procedures. TRUE FALSE

13) Using the table of contents in a book to locate specific information is an example of which type of navigation?

      A. linear navigation
      B. conditional branching
      C. hypertext "jumps"

14) The nonlinear, nonsequential arrangement of information that seeks to replicate the way the human brain thinks best defines:

      A. hypertext.
      B. computer-assisted instruction.
      C. conditional branching.
      D. simulation.

15) Competition plays an important role in which form of computer-assisted instruction?

      A. drill and practice
      B. tutorials
      C. educational games
      D. simulations

16) Tutorial writers often divide their instructional content into brief, "self-standing" components that deal with a limited amount of information. These components are called . . .

      A. cognitive breaks.
      B. modules.
      C. nodes.
      D. hypertext "jumps."

17) Computer-based tutorials are always more cost-efficient than traditional classroom instruction. TRUE FALSE

18) Which of the following is NOT a characteristic of successful play (and successful learning)?

    A. active engagement of the participant
    B. strategy building to complete tasks
    C. personal commitment to game/learning context
    D. repetitive reinforcement of facts

19) "Digitized approximations of real situations, tasks, and procedures" best describes . . .

    A. drill and practice.
    B. tutorials.
    C. educational games.
    D. simulations.

20) The best tools for teaching complex processes or procedures, decision making, and problem solving are . . .

    A. drill and practice.
    B. tutorials.
    C. educational games.
    D. simulations.

21) The simulation scenario should be "self-revising"—that is, the scenario should be modified after each decision point to reflect changes brought on by the learner's choices. TRUE FALSE

22) Taken together, all of the choices made by the learner in a simulation form a . . .

    A. decision point.
    B. decision scenario.
    C. decision path.
    D. decision evaluation.

Jigsaw Team Collaboration

"Jigsaw Review"

Cooperative learning strategies meet with great success in classrooms. In cooperative learning, students in a class are assigned to heterogeneous groups called "teams." Team combinations and sizes can vary greatly. Team members work together, helping one another, to learn the assigned material. In this activity, you will be part of a "jigsaw" team. Together, your group will cover a large amount of material in a short amount of time.

Directions:
1) Work with your fellow classmates to form a team of five to seven members.
2) Each member of your team should select a Web site from the "Evaluating Instructional Software" section on the companion CD-ROM, in the "Online Resources" section.
3) Each member of your team should access their selected Web site and complete the review form below.
4) After reviewing the sites, each member of the team should read their review to fellow members.

Your Instructional Software Web Site Review

List the URL: http://_____

Title of the Web site: _____

Describe the main idea or message of the site.

_____

_____

_____

_____

What was the most valuable insight regarding instructional software found at this site?

_____

_____

_____

_____

_____

_____

_____

_____

Evaluating Instructional Software Project

ACTIVITY INSTRUCTIONS

STEP ONE:
From the CD-ROM home page, select the "Evaluating Instructional Software" icon. Next, scroll down to the "Interactive Web Exercises" section and click the "Educational Software Evaluation Exercise" option.

In this section you will evaluate an instructional software title using the software evaluation form on the companion CD-ROM for this workbook. Check with your instructor about obtaining the necessary software. Your instructor will provide the software on CD-ROMs and/or in computer labs. Try to select a software title that is designed for a grade level or subject you would like to teach or are currently teaching.

If you do not have access to any instructional software titles, consider evaluating free "demos" of popular software online. Locate the software tools using one of the search engines found on the "Interactive Exercises" page on the CD-ROM. Search for "free educational software." Many companies offer free downloads of their software. Follow the installation instructions found at their Web sites. Be sure to read the licensing agreements and system requirements before attempting to install the software. Good luck!

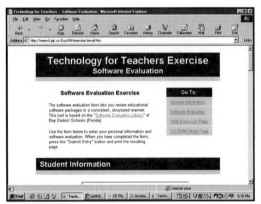

STEP TWO:

Product Information Instructions:

Fill out the general information at the top of the form. Scroll down until you see "Product." Type the title of the software you are reviewing in this field.

Click every checkbox that applies for Grade Level, Learning Approach, Intended Audience, and System Requirements. You will have to scroll down the screen to access these categories.

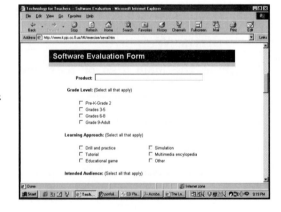

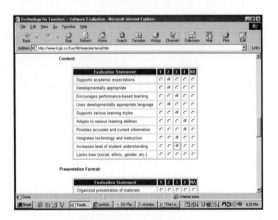

STEP THREE:

Evaluation Criteria Ranking Instructions:

Read the on-screen evaluation instructions carefully. Rank each statement 1 to 4: 1 for strongly disagree, 2 for disagree, 3 for agree, and 4 for strongly agree. Select "NA" if the statement is not applicable. Use the comments field for additional evaluation. When you have completed the form, click the "Submit" button and print the resulting page. Include the printed evaluation in the portfolio workbook.

Evaluating Instructional Software

Structured Reflection Journal

Write several paragraphs on your thoughts and opinions regarding "Evaluating Instructional Software." Check with your instructor for the desired length of your response. Consider responding to:

* What learning objectives are most appropriate for drill and practice? What are the benefits of simulations?

* How can you fight boredom in computerized drill and practice?

* What major issues should a teacher consider when evaluating instructional software?

* What questions should a teacher ask when evaluating educational Web sites ? What is the missing ingredient in most educational Web sites, and why is it important?

JOURNAL INSTRUCTIONS

STEP ONE:
1) Insert the *Technology for Teachers* CD-ROM.
2) If the CD-ROM does not auto-load, launch your Web browser and open the "index.htm" file on the CD-ROM. This file can be found in the ROOT folder of the CD-ROM. (That's the first folder that opens when you double click on the icon to look at your CD-ROM drive contents.) This page will load in your browser.
3) Click the "Evaluating Instructional Software" icon.
4) Scroll to the "Interactive Exercises" section of this page and click the desired question under "Structured Journal Exercises."

STEP TWO:
Click in each field of the "Structured Journal" form and enter the following:

1) Type your name (first name, then last).
2) Type the name of this course.
3) Type the name of your school or college.
4) Type your journal entry in the "Comments" field. Entries can be up to 20 pages of text in length and can be copied and pasted to the form from a word processor. Remember to place a "double-spaced" return between paragraphs.

STEP THREE:
Submit Entry

Click the button located at the bottom of the form.
This will produce a Web page in your browser with your comments. Click the "Print" button in your browser. This will print your journal entry.

Place this journal entry inside the portfolio workbook to complete the assignment. Your instructor will give you due dates for each activity.

Open Reflection Journal

Questions for Reflection Journals

The purpose of the "open reflection" exercise is to encourage you to document your insights and questions about this topic. This record of your thoughts can serve as a "springboard" for reflective thinking—the beginning of an "internal dialogue" with your own thoughts as you gain more knowledge and experience. While this exercise is truly open-ended (that is, you can enter any comment you desire), consider writing about broad questions like the following:

- What is the most important lesson you have learned in this section? Why?
- What are your personal strengths and weaknesses in this area?
- How would you implement what you have learned about this topic in a classroom? What specific strategies would you use? What type of lesson plans would you develop?
- What is the greatest obstacle for using this type of technology in traditional classrooms?
- What questions remain unanswered about this topic?

JOURNAL INSTRUCTIONS
STEP ONE:

From the CD-ROM home page, select the "Evaluating Instructional Software" icon. Then scroll down to the "Interactive Web Exercises" section and click the "Reflection Journal" option.

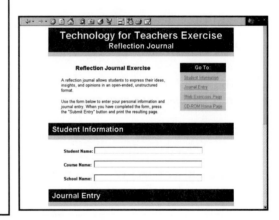

STEP TWO:

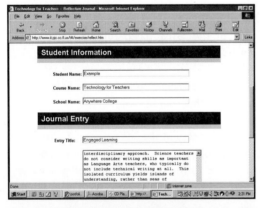

Click in each field on the form that appears, and type the following:

Type in your name and the name of your course and school. In the "Entry Title" field, type a meaningful title for your entry. Click in the comment field directly below and begin typing your journal entry. Remember, you can write your reflection in a word processing program, run spelling and grammar checking, and "cut-and-paste" your work into the comment field.

STEP THREE:

Submit Entry

Click the button located at the bottom of the form. This will produce a Web page in your browser with your comments. Click the "Print" button in your browser. This will print your journal entry.

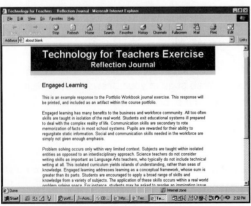

Place this journal entry inside the portfolio workbook to complete the assignment. Your instructor will give you due dates for each activity.

Classroom Management Strategies

School districts everywhere are caught up in the "mad rush" toward technology. Board policies and legislative mandates call for equal access to technology tools—a fair and equitable distribution of resources—for all students. A virtual "feeding frenzy" of technology purchases is filling classrooms and laboratories with computers and monitors. But in many cases, no real plan for using these technology tools—for achieving real educational change with technology as a catalyst—is in place. Classroom management strategies, facilities design, and long-range planning are absolutely necessary if these technology expenditures are to make any real educational difference.

To introduce "Classroom Management Strategies," the *Technology for Teachers* CD-ROM includes the following materials:

> **"Classroom Management and Facilities Design: Practical Guidelines and Suggestions"** provides several creative strategies for maximizing limited technology resources for effective instruction. This is a "must see" presentation for every classroom instructor.

> **"Classroom Design 'Cutout' Sheet: A Participatory Exercise in Classroom Design"** allows you to plan classroom layout and technology resources for the effective integration of computer technologies into instruction.

> **"Planning Considerations: Information Needs and Instructional Challenges"** offers guidelines for long-range planning that seek to equip and empower teachers for technology-enhanced instruction.

To access these materials, load the CD-ROM, select the "Classroom Management Strategies" icon, and click the desired article title.

In addition, this portfolio workbook contains the following learning activities:

> **Review Questions: Classroom Management Strategies**
> **Key Concepts Exercise: Classroom Management Strategies**
> **Online Activity: Technology-Planning Web Sites**
> **"Hands-On" Activity: Classroom Design Interview/Reflection**
> **Structured Reflection Journal**
> **"Hands-On" Activity: "Cut-and-Paste" Classroom Design Project**
> **Open Reflection Journal**

Classroom Management Strategies

The purchase of classroom computers and presentation equipment does not guarantee the effective integration of technology into teaching and learning. Classroom management strategies, facilities design, and long-range technology planning are equally necessary to realize technology's potential for education.

SECTIONS:

* Classroom Management and Facilities Design
* Planning Considerations
* Classroom Design "Cutout" Sheet

Section Review Questions

1) In a "one computer classroom" the computer is typically found . . .
    a) at a student desk.   b) right next to a chalkboard.
    c) in an independent study carrel.   d) at the teacher's desk.

2) Classroom environments where students move from area to area, completing related or thematic tasks, are called . . .
    a) traditional classrooms.   b) workstation rotation environments.
    c) independent study areas.   d) enhanced environments.

3) Which of the following is NOT an advantage of a workstation rotation learning environment?
    a) The teacher becomes a facilitator, guide, and co-learner.
    b) Workstations are organized so that all students encounter a variety of learning tasks.
    c) Workstations appeal to a variety of learning styles.
    d) Such environments take the teacher less time to design, leaving more time for students.

4) An environment where a common theme is explored at each station is a . . .
    a) resource design.   b) independent study design.   c) traditional design.   d) static design.

5) As personal computers became more popular, many schools chose to consolidate available computers into _____ _____.

6) As computer software _____, labs no longer became the dominion of the business division.

7) Areas where strategic rooms are equipped for specific teaching styles are called
_____ _____.

8) A team of teachers can share facilities based upon _____ _____.

9) Staff members need to plan together to share and optimize existing resources in schools.
   TRUE   FALSE

10) School administrators should NOT play a major role in designing and equipping classrooms.
   TRUE   FALSE

Key Concepts: Short Answers

1) Describe the physical set up of a "traditional classroom."

_____
_____
_____
_____

2) What would a classroom set up as a "workstation rotation" environment look like?

_____
_____
_____
_____

3) Describe the "resource design" model for classrooms.

_____
_____
_____
_____

4) What are several advantages of computer labs?

_____
_____
_____
_____

5) What is a "multi-purposed" area?

_____
_____
_____
_____

6) What are several advantages of creating "purposed areas" within schools?

_____
_____
_____
_____

7) What might be some disadvantages of this approach?

_____
_____
_____
_____

Technology-Planning Web Sites

Technology Planning for Schools

No teacher or classroom exists in isolation. Implementing technology—integrating computer technologies into the daily acts of teaching and learning—is an issue for the entire school or school district to consider. The advent of network technologies and access to the Internet in schools has brought attention to the need for school-wide technology planning. Such planning is often formalized, recorded in a document, and placed on the Web for other schools and interested individuals. In this exercise, you will identify and summarize the components of an effective technology plan.

Directions:

1) Select a Web site from the "Classroom Management Strategies" section on the companion CD-ROM. Look in the "Online Resources" section.
2) Identify the elements that the authors list as effective components of a technology plan. (Example: establishing time frames, committing to staff development, etc.)
3) List and describe these elements below and on the following page.

Components of a Technology Plan

List the URL: http://_____

_____

_____

_____

_____

_____

_____

_____

_____

_____

_____

_____

_____

_____

_____

Components of a Technology Plan

Classroom Management Strategies

Classroom Design Interview/Reflection

The models of classroom management and design found on the CD-ROM are certainly not the only options to consider. Teachers must respond to the unique demands of their students, schools, and community. We must expand our experience if we are to gain a new appreciation for classroom design. This activity will require a visit to a local school. Check with your instructor for additional details before following each of the steps below.

1) Contact a school in your local community. Try to select one with a grade level and/or subject area you are interested in teaching. If you are currently teaching, consider visiting a classroom from a different grade level or subject area.

2) Schedule an interview with a practicing teacher in your area of interest. Ask for only 15 minutes of their time. Teachers are extremely busy, with many responsibilities demanding their attention. In some schools, an administrator or principal approval will be required. Tell your contact that you are researching classroom management and design strategies for your course work.

3) Be sure to check in with the main office of the school or campus you are visiting as soon as you arrive. Obtain the needed guest identifications, parking permits, etc. Do not visit a school or campus uninvited.

4) On the next page, you will find a brief interview form to complete. Introduce yourself and move quickly to the survey.

5) As you complete the survey, take a moment to look around. Make mental notes on the following:

    * Look for images and information on the walls of the classroom. Is student work displayed?
    * What is the overall condition of equipment and furniture?
    * Is the heating and/or cooling of the area sufficient?
    * Are exits and entryways unobstructed?
    * If there are any computers, do they appear to be accessible to students?
    * Where is the teacher's desk located?
    * Are student materials neatly stored?
    * Is there an overhead projector in the classroom?
    * How are the desks and/or tables arranged?
    * What do you think the students are currently investigating or studying? (Don't ask.)
    * Is this a passive or active learning environment?

6) After you complete the interview, record your post-interview observations on the form. Recall your mental notes on the above questions or any other observations you feel were important about classroom management and design.

Classroom Management Strategies

Classroom Design Interview

Student Name_____ Course Number and Section _____

Name of Teacher Interviewed_____ School _____

Date of Interview ____ / ____ / ____   Time of Interview _____

Interview Questions:

1) What subject(s) and/or grade level(s) do you teach?

_____

2) How long have you been teaching? _____ How long in this grade/subject? _____

3) How many students do you teach each day? _____

4) Do you share a room or rooms with other teachers? _____ How many? _____

5) Describe the arrangement of the student desks or work areas in your classroom and why you
   have arranged them in this particular fashion.

_____
_____
_____
_____
_____
_____

6) Are there any computers in the classroom, and if so how many? _____
   If not, do students in your class use or have access to computers used in your grade/subject?

_____

7) What is the average age of the computer(s)?

_____

8) Describe how students use computers in your grade/subject area.

_____
_____
_____

9) What is the greatest challenge in your classroom? _____

_____
_____

10) Why did you enter the teaching profession?

_____
_____
_____

Classroom Design Reflection

Write several paragraphs on your thoughts from your interview. Comment on the responses to the interview questions and the mental notes you made during your visit. Respond to these questions as assigned by your instructor.

*Compare the classroom you visited in your interview with other classrooms you have visited.

*What teaching philosophy was used in the classroom you visited?

*What strategies did you witness during the classroom visit that you hope to implement in your own classes?

*What were the strengths and weaknesses of the design of the classroom you visited?

*Did you feel that the classroom you visited was an innovative environment? Why?

JOURNAL INSTRUCTIONS

STEP ONE:
1) Insert the *Technology for Teachers* CD-ROM.
2) If the CD-ROM does not auto-load, launch your Web browser and open the "index.htm" file on the CD-ROM. This file can be found in the ROOT folder of the CD-ROM. (That's the first folder that opens when you double click on the icon to look at your CD-ROM drive contents.) This page will load in your browser.
3) Click the "Classroom Management Strategies" icon.
4) Scroll to the "Interactive Exercises" section of this page and click the desired question under "Structured Journal Exercises."

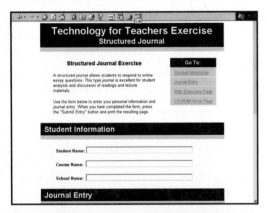

STEP TWO:
Click in each field of the "Structured Journal" form and enter the following:

1) Type your name (first name, then last).
2) Type the name of this course.
3) Type the name of your school or college.
4) Type your journal entry in the "Comments" field. Entries can be up to 20 pages of text in length and can be copied and pasted to the form from a word processor. Remember to place a "double-spaced" return between paragraphs.

STEP THREE: Submit Entry

Click the button located at the bottom of the form. This will produce a Web page in your browser with your comments. Click the "Print" button in your browser. This will print your journal entry.

Place this journal entry inside the portfolio workbook to complete the assignment. Your instructor will give you due dates for each activity.

"Cut-and-Paste" Classroom Design Project

DIRECTIONS: The gray area below represents the average size of a classroom constructed to support 24 -30 students. The items surrounding the area are proportional in size. Copy this page with a copy machine. (You can also print a copy from the CD-ROM by selecting the "Classroom Management Strategies" icon and clicking on the "Classroom Design Cutout Sheet" option.) Use scissors and glue to "cut-and-paste" these items into your ideal learning environment. Make sure that you create a classroom that supports 24-30 students. Leave room for walking, and don't forget the doors.

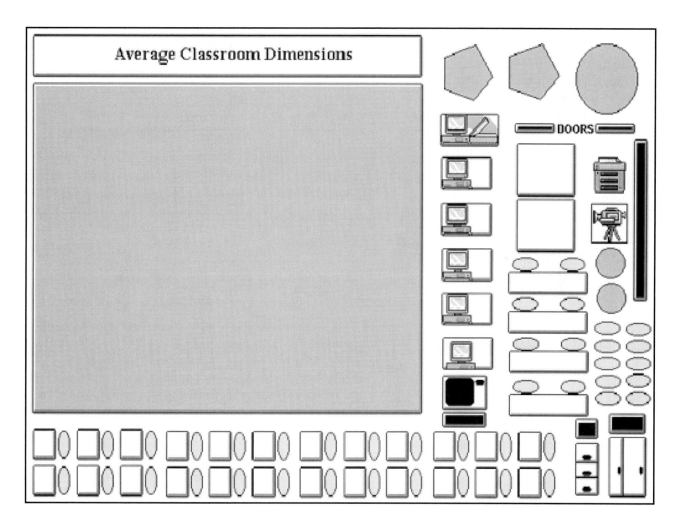

Write one paragraph describing your design and why you chose to arrange your classroom in that particular manner. Turn in your completed classroom design and description to your instructor. Your work should be included as an artifact in the portfolio workbook.

Open Reflection Journal

Questions for Reflection Journals

The purpose of the "open reflection" exercise is to encourage you to document your insights and questions about this topic. This record of your thoughts can serve as a "springboard" for reflective thinking—the beginning of an "internal dialogue" with your own thoughts as you gain more knowledge and experience. While this exercise is truly open-ended (that is, you can enter any comment you desire), consider writing about broad questions like the following:

- What is the most important lesson you have learned in this section? Why?
- What are your personal strengths and weaknesses in this area?
- How would you implement what you have learned about this topic in a classroom? What specific strategies would you use? What type of lesson plans would you develop?
- What is the greatest obstacle for using this type of technology in traditional classrooms?
- What questions remain unanswered about this topic?

JOURNAL INSTRUCTIONS
STEP ONE:
From the CD-ROM home page, select the "Classroom Management Strategies" icon. Next, scroll down to the "Interactive Web Exercises" section and click the "Reflection Journal" option.

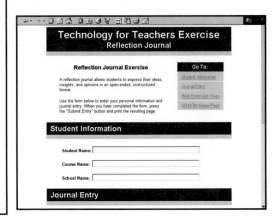

STEP TWO:

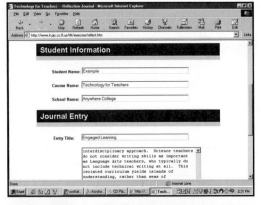

Click in each field on the form that appears, and type the following:

Type in your name and the name of your course and school. In the "Entry Title" field, type a meaningful title for your entry. Click in the comment field directly below and begin typing your journal entry. Remember, you can write your reflection in a word processing program, run spelling and grammar checking, and "cut-and-paste" your work into the comment field.

STEP THREE:

Click the button located at the bottom of the form. This will produce a Web page in your browser with your comments. Click the "Print" button in your browser. This will print your journal entry.

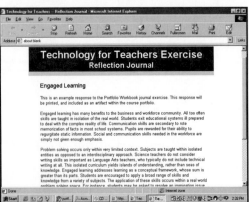

Place this journal entry inside the portfolio workbook to complete the assignment. Your instructor will give you due dates for each activity.

Implementing Presentation Technologies

For many instructors, the first step in integrating technology tools into their teaching is the use of computer presentations to enhance traditional lectures. While this step falls short of the ultimate goal of using technology to actively engage students in learner-centered activities, it is nevertheless an important step that "breaks the ice" for many instructors—a "first step" in experimenting with technology as a normal part of everyday instruction. Presentation software and a variety of projection devices are increasingly becoming standard tools for instructors.

To introduce "Implementing Presentation Technologies," the *Technology for Teachers* CD-ROM includes the following materials:

"Effective Classroom Presentations: The 'Nuts and Bolts' of Presentation Building" addresses all aspects of computerized presentation building—the combination of text, graphics, color, and multimedia to effectively communicate a message in a computer presentation.

"Presentation Technologies: It Starts with a Piece of Chalk . . ." surveys the range of presentation technologies available to classroom instructors—from the simplest chalkboard to the complex "smart classrooms" and video projection equipment.

To access these materials, load the CD-ROM, select the "Implementing Presentation Technologies" icon, and click the desired article title.

In addition, this portfolio workbook contains the following learning activities:

Review Questions: Implementing Presentation Technologies
15 Terms Every Teacher Should Know
Key Article Quiz: "Effective Classroom Presentations"
Online Activity: Shopping for Presentation Equipment
"Hands-On" Activity: Building a Classroom Presentation
Structured Reflection Journal
Open Reflection Journal

Implementing Presentation Technologies

For many instructors, the first step in integrating new media and technologies into their teaching is the computerized presentation. Presentation software and projection devices add new life to the traditional delivery of information.

SECTIONS:

*Effective Classroom
 Presentations
*Presentation Technologies

Section Review Questions

1) When a presenter projects a slide of information in a presentation, the viewer must . . .
   a) select among multiple stimuli received.
   b) recognize and comprehend patterns in the stimuli.
   c) access long-term memory for related knowledge.
   d) all of the above.

2) What controls which information flows into short-term memory and which information is immediately discarded?
   a) long-term memory   b) the external environment
   c) selective attention   d) enhanced environments

3) Psychological tests reveal that the average short-term human memory can retain . . .
   a) 5-7 pieces of information.   b) 3-5 pieces of information.   c) 7-9 pieces of information.

4) A practical guide for presenting information in a constrained time period is to build one slide for. . .
   a) every 5 minutes.   b) every 2 minutes.   c) every 30 seconds.   d) every 10 seconds.

5) Predesigned screen formats that make all preliminary design decisions for the presenter are called . . .
   a) backgrounds   b) objects.   c) patterns.   d) templates.

6) _____ is a visual outlining technique that graphically describes every slide in a presentation.

7) Each presentation consists of three segments: an introduction, the _____ , and a
   _____ .

8) Psychologists tell us that audience members show the sharpest attention at the _____
   of a presentation.

9) The use of multimedia always improves the effectiveness of a presentation.   TRUE   FALSE

10) The most important element in the communication chain is the speaker.   TRUE   FALSE

15 Terms Nobody Wants to Memorize, but Every Teacher Should Know

1) information chunking:

_____

_____

2) cognitive breaks:

_____

_____

3) digitized sound:

_____

_____

4) projection devices:

_____

_____

5) text legibility:

_____

_____

6) text readability:

_____

_____

7) parallelism:

_____

_____

8) serif and sans-serif fonts:

_____

_____

9) font substitution:

_____

10) color saturation:

_____

_____

11) bitmaps:

_____

_____

12) line drawings:

_____

13) graphic resolution:

_____

_____

14) white space:

_____

15) "high-low" graphs:

_____

_____

These questions are drawn from the "**Effective Classroom Presentations: The 'Nuts and Bolts' of Presentation Building**" article on the CD-ROM.

1. When a presenter uses headings, subheadings, main "bullet" text, and "sub-bullets" to group and rank the relative importance of information, we refer to this arrangement as . . .

    A. hierarchical organization.
    B. cognitive breaks.
    C. information chunking.
    D. cueing systems.

2. Which of the following is NOT a tool used in the hierarchical organization of information in presentation slides?

    A. differing text sizes for headings and bullets
    B. positioning and grouping of screen elements
    C. hypertext arrangement of information and links
    D. use of "white" space between headings and bullets

3. The fact that the human brain retains short lists (less than 5 to 7 items) best calls for which practice when building presentations?

    A. cueing systems
    B. conditional branching
    C. hierarchical organization
    D. information chunking

4. While humans cannot seem to effectively memorize long lists of information, they appear quite capable of grasping a large number of short lists. TRUE FALSE

5. The presenter should be able to sum up the main message in a single statement, and this statement should serve as the guiding principle for all sections of the presentation. TRUE FALSE

6. A good rule of thumb for presenting information in a constrained time period is to build one slide for every _____ minutes/of presentation time.

  A. 1
  B. 2
  C. 5
  D. 10

7. A presentation "slide master" refers to a . . .

    A. template that provides a framework of objects and colors.
    B. predefined guide for presentation content.
    C. highly skilled presenter or educator.
    D. software package for building presentations.

8. What maximum number of templates should be used for building effective slide presentations?

    A. one
    B. two
    C. five
    D. ten

9. A visual outlining technique that graphically (sometimes very crudely) describes each slide in a presentation is called a . . .

    A. slide master.
    B. presentation template.
    C. visual cue.
    D. storyboard.

10. Typically, a presentation's introduction consists of all of the following EXCEPT . . .

    A. title slide.
    B. outcomes slide.
    C. overview slide.
    D. summary slide.

11. Shifts in activities during a presentation that allow the audience to approach information in a different setting or mode are called . . .

    A. verbal cues.
    B. cognitive breaks.
    C. information chunks.
    D. summary conclusions.

12. Text visibility—the ease of distinguishing the characters of the text from the background—is largely a function of . . .

    A. contrasting text and background colors.
    B. font selection and size.
    C. room size and lighting.
    D. seating arrangements.

13. Text legibility refers to . . .

    A. the ease of distinguishing text and background colors.
    B. the amount of text on each line of a presentation.
    C. the ability to distinguish between characters in the chosen font face.
    D. the contrast between text and graphics on a slide.

14. A complete set of alphabetical, numerical, punctuation, and special characters is called . . .

    A. font size.
    B. font style.
    C. font face.
    D. font spacing.

15. Presenting each item in a "bullet list" in the same grammatical structure is called . . .

    A. parallelism.
    B. font substitution.
    C. text chunking.
    D. readability.

16. Normal capitalization—capitalizing only proper nouns and the first word of each line—is best for the body text of a presentation. TRUE FALSE

17. Sans-serif fonts have thin extensions that project from the main strokes in each character of a font face. TRUE FALSE

18. It is almost always best to avoid outlined, shadowed, and script font faces in presentations. TRUE FALSE

19. What occurs when the fonts used to develop a presentation are not installed on the computer used to make the presentation?

    A. text chunking
    B. font substitution
    C. improper parallelism
    D. loss of information

20. "Blues" and "greens" tend to excite the eye, drawing attention immediately to an object, while "reds" are more subdued and relax the eye of the viewer, making them better choices for background colors. TRUE FALSE

21. A presentation's color scheme involves all of the following EXCEPT . . .

    A. background color.
    B. accent colors.
    C. text (or foreground) color.
    D. saturation color.

22. Bitmap graphics can be successfully resized without a loss of quality whereas "vector" graphics (line drawings) are distorted when resized. TRUE FALSE

23. Which type of graph best shows the change of data over time?

    A. bar graph
    B. high-low graph
    C. pie graph
    D. "exploding" pie graph

24. Which type of graph best shows proportional relationships among a set of numbers (i.e., smallest to largest)?

    A. pie graph
    B. line graph
    C. area graph
    D. high-low graph

25. Simplified symbolic graphics often focus the viewer's attention on the specific details that concern the presenter better than more complicated "photo-realistic" images. TRUE FALSE

Implementing Presentation Technologies

Shopping for Presentation Equipment

Selecting an appropriate presentation technology is a major step in creating a technology-enhanced classroom. As an instructor, you may well one day be asked to recommend projection equipment for purchase to your supervisor or principal. In this exercise, you will use the Web to locate and price the equipment listed in the categories below.

Directions:

1) Connect to an Internet search engine. Use the "Web Search Tools" list of the search engine found on the "Interactive Web Exercises" section of the CD-ROM.
2) Type in the device category as listed below.
3) Follow the links produced by the search engine until you locate a specific device from a specific manufacturer. Locate at least three devices for each category.
4) Complete the information in the table below.

Device Category	Manufacturer	Model	Price
1) 27" television	A)		
	B)		
	C)		
2) scan converter	A) Good Systems	Television T3 Pro PC	$249.95
	B)		
	C)		
3) LCD projection panel	A)		
	B)		
	C)		
4) video-data projector	A)		
	B)		
	C)		
5) 27" or larger computer monitor	A)		
	B)		
	C)		

Implementing Presentation Technologies

Building a Classroom Presentation

Many educators first embrace computer technology when making classroom presentations. In this exercise, you will plan a presentation using the storyboarding techniques introduced earlier. If presentation software, such as Microsoft PowerPoint or Adobe Persuasion, is available, we strongly recommend that you use the storyboards you have developed to build a computerized presentation.

If at all possible, present your completed work before an audience, perhaps your class. The best experience for the presenter is to present as often as possible in a variety of settings to a variety of audiences.

The following pages provide you with templates to create a storyboard for your work. Complete the storyboard using the guidelines on this page.

STEP ONE: Select your topic. The topic of the presentation can focus on the subject matter or grade level you would like to teach or are currently teaching. Try to choose a topic with which you are already familiar for this exercise. Check with your instructor for approval of topics before beginning work.

STEP TWO: Complete a storyboard on paper using the template pages in this workbook. Copy additional pages as needed or print the templates from the "Interactive Web Exercises" section of the CD-ROM. Click on the "Storyboard Templates" option. An effective presentation will include:

>   Title Page
>   List of Topics (outline)
>   Learning Outcomes Page
>   Content Pages (containing subject matter)
>   Summary of Ideas (conclusion)

STEP THREE: Complete notes for content pages. Enter the text bullets for each content slide. Make sure each bullet is grammatically correct and parallel. Also, include presentation notes to "script" the delivery of the presentation.

STEP FOUR: Gather the media. Refer to the *Elements of Multimedia* and *Harvesting the Web* articles in the "Multimedia Student Authoring" section on the CD.

STEP FIVE: Use presentation software to create your presentation. The "Auto Content Wizard" in Microsoft PowerPoint is an excellent place to begin. Check with your instructor for availability and further instructions.

STEP SIX: Include your work in the portfolio workbook.

Presentation Storyboard

Student Name: _____ Course # _____ Section # _____

TITLE SLIDE

Write your title here . . .

Author:

Slide Media List:

🔊 Sounds

Music _____

_____

Voice _____

_____

📷 Video _____

_____

_____

Other _____

_____

Notes:
_____
_____
_____
_____
_____
_____
_____
_____
_____
_____
_____
_____

Presentation Storyboard

OUTLINE SLIDE

Write your slide title here . . .

Write the titles of each slide or major points of your presentation below . . .

Notes:

_____
_____
_____
_____
_____
_____
_____
_____
_____
_____
_____
_____
_____
_____

Slide Media List:

Sounds
Music _____

_____

Voice _____

_____

Video _____

_____

_____

Other _____

_____

Presentation Storyboard

LEARNING OUTCOMES SLIDE

Write your slide title here . . .

List specific outcomes that your learners will demonstrate after this presentation . . .

-
-
-
-
-
-

Notes:

_____
_____
_____
_____
_____
_____
_____
_____
_____
_____
_____
_____
_____
_____

Slide Media List:

Sounds
music _____
_____

voice _____
_____

Video _____
_____
_____

Other _____
_____

Presentation Storyboard

CONTENT SLIDE

Write your slide title here . . .

Image Area:
Pictures and clip-art are placed here.

Cut-and-paste an image here.

Or list file name:
_____

Bullets: Write key points below . . .

○ _____

○ _____

○ _____

○ _____

○ _____

Notes:
_____
_____
_____
_____
_____
_____
_____
_____
_____
_____
_____
_____
_____
_____

Slide Media List:

🔊 Sounds
Music _____
_____

Voice _____
_____

📹 Video _____

_____

Other _____
_____

Presentation Storyboard

CONTENT SLIDE

Write your slide title here . . .

Bullets: Write key points below . . .

Image Area:
Pictures and clip-art are placed here.

Cut-and-paste an image here.

Or list file name:
_____

Notes:
_____
_____
_____
_____
_____
_____
_____
_____
_____
_____
_____
_____
_____
_____

Slide Media List:

Sounds
Music _____
_____

Voice _____
_____

Video _____
_____

Other _____
_____

Presentation Storyboard

CONTENT SLIDE

Write your slide title here . . .

Bullets: Write key points below . . .

Bullets: Write key points below . . .

Notes:

_____
_____
_____
_____
_____
_____
_____
_____
_____
_____
_____
_____

Slide Media List:

Sounds
Music _____

_____

Voice _____

_____

Video _____

_____
_____

Other _____

_____

Presentation Storyboard

CONTENT SLIDE

Write your slide title here . . .

Image Area:
Pictures and clip-art are placed here.

Cut-and-paste an image here.

Or list file name:
_____

Bullets: Write key points below . . .

Notes:
_____
_____
_____
_____
_____
_____
_____
_____
_____
_____
_____
_____
_____

Slide Media List:

Sounds
Music _____
_____

Voice _____
_____

Video _____
_____
_____

Other _____
_____

Presentation Storyboard

CONTENT SLIDE

Write your slide title here . . .

Bullets: Write key points below . . .

Image Area:
Pictures and clip-art are placed here.

Cut-and-paste an image here.

Or list file name:
_____

Notes:

_____
_____
_____
_____
_____
_____
_____
_____
_____
_____
_____
_____
_____
_____

Slide Media List:

Sounds
Music _____
_____

Voice _____
_____

Video _____
_____
_____

Other _____
_____

Presentation Storyboard

CONTENT SLIDE

Write your slide title here...

Image Area: Place pictures and clip-art here.

Image Area: Place pictures and clip-art here.

Or list filename:_____

Or list filename:_____

Bullets: Write key points below . . .

○

○

Notes:
_____
_____
_____
_____
_____
_____
_____
_____
_____
_____
_____
_____
_____
_____
_____

Slide Media List:

🔊 Sounds
Music _____
_____

Voice _____
_____

📹 Video _____
_____
_____

Other _____
_____

Presentation Storyboard

CONCLUSION SLIDE

Write your slide title here . . .

Bullets: Review each of the major points of the presentation below . . .

Notes:

_____
_____
_____
_____
_____
_____
_____
_____
_____
_____
_____
_____
_____
_____

Slide Media List:

🔊 Sounds

Music _____
_____

Voice _____
_____

📹 Video _____
_____
_____

Other _____
_____

Structured Reflection Journal

Write several paragraphs on your thoughts and opinions regarding "Integrating Presentation Technologies." Check with your instructor for the desired length of your response. Consider responding to:

- What are the benefits of integrating presentation technologies into a classroom?

- What presentation devices and solutions are available, and in what settings are they appropriately implemented?

- Describe the presentation technologies projected to be widely available in the near future. How will such devices have impact in the classroom?

- To what does the term "screen-agers" refer? Why is this important in considering presentation technologies?

JOURNAL INSTRUCTIONS

STEP ONE
1) Insert the *Technology for Teachers* CD-ROM.
2) If the CD-ROM does not auto-load, launch your Web browser and open the "index.htm" file on the CD-ROM. This file can be found in the ROOT folder of the CD-ROM. (That's the first folder that opens when you double click on the icon to look at your CD-ROM drive contents.) This page will load in your browser.
3) Click the "Implementing Presentation Technologies" icon.
4) Scroll to the "Interactive Exercises" section of this page and click the desired question under "Structured Journal Exercises."

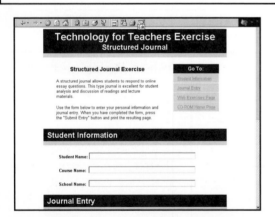

STEP TWO:
Click in each field of the "Structured Journal" form and enter the following:

1) Type your name (first name, then last).
2) Type the name of this course.
3) Type the name of your school or college.
4) Type your journal entry in the "Comments" field. Entries can be up to 20 pages of text in length and can be copied and pasted to the form from a word processor. Remember to place a "double-spaced" return between paragraphs.

STEP THREE: Submit Entry

Click the button located at the bottom of the form. This will produce a Web page in your browser with your comments. Click the "Print" button in your browser. This will print your journal entry.

Place this journal entry inside the portfolio workbook to complete the assignment. Your instructor will give you due dates for each activity.

Open Reflection Journal

Questions for Reflection Journals

The purpose of the "open reflection" exercise is to encourage you to document your insights and questions about this topic. This record of your thoughts can serve as a "springboard" for reflective thinking—the beginning of an "internal dialogue" with your own thoughts as you gain more knowledge and experience. While this exercise is truly open-ended (that is, you can enter any comment you desire), consider writing about broad questions like the following:

- What is the most important lesson you have learned in this section? Why?
- What are your personal strengths and weaknesses in this area?
- How would you implement what you have learned about this topic in a classroom? What specific strategies would you use? What type of lesson plans would you develop?
- What is the greatest obstacle for using this type of technology in traditional classrooms?
- What questions remain unanswered about this topic?

JOURNAL INSTRUCTIONS
STEP ONE:

From the CD-ROM home page, select the "Implementing Presentation Technologies" icon. Next, scroll down to the "Interactive Web Exercises" section and click the "Reflection Journal" option.

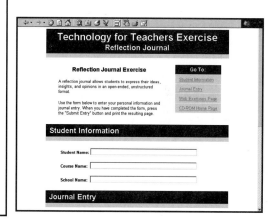

STEP TWO:

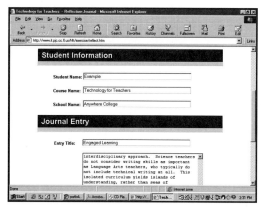

Click in each field on the form that appears, and type the following:

Type in your name and the name of your course and school. In the "Entry Title" field, type a meaningful title for your entry. Click in the comment field directly below and begin typing your journal entry. Remember, you can write your reflection in a word processing program, run spelling and grammar checking, and "cut-and-paste" your work into the comment field.

STEP THREE:

Click the button located at the bottom of the form. This will produce a Web page in your browser with your comments. Click the "Print" button in your browser. This will print your journal entry.

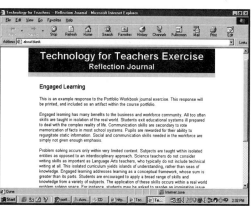

Place this journal entry inside the portfolio workbook to complete the assignment. Your instructor will give you due dates for each activity.

Measuring Student Performance

As instructors embrace new models of teaching, they often experiment with alternative means of assessing student performance. Traditional objective testing, while fine for measuring comprehension of simple factual information, does not—and can not—successfully measure student problem-solving, decision-making, or other higher-order thinking skills. More and more instructors are turning to performance-based assessment for measuring student progress—assessment models that focus on "real-world" skills learned and evaluated in "real-world" settings.

To introduce "Measuring Student Performance," the *Technology for Teachers* CD-ROM includes the following materials:

> **"Authentic Assessment: Not an Alternative"** offers insights into this essential model of evaluation for measuring student performance.

> **"Lesson Plan Format for Micro-Teach: A Step-by-Step Guide"** provides a step-by-step guide to help instructors plan successful lessons.

To access these materials, load the CD-ROM, select the "Measuring Student Performance" icon, and click the desired article title.

In addition, this portfolio workbook contains the following learning activities:

Review Questions: Measuring Student Performance
"Hands-On" Activity: The Power of Student Portfolios
Online Activity: Locating Exemplary Lesson Plans
Online Activity: Accountability and Lesson Planning
Structured Reflection Journal
Open Reflection Journal

Measuring Student Performance

The new models of active, engaged learning call for new models of assessment. Teachers are moving away from objective testing, toward authentic, performance-based assessment of student progress. These new assessment models focus on "real-world" skills, learned and assessed in "real-world" settings.

SECTIONS:

*Authentic Assessment:
 Not an Alternative
*Lesson Plan Format for
 Micro-Teach: A Step-by-Step Guide

Section Review Questions

1) The most common classroom assessment is consistent with . . .
 a) cognitive learning theory.　　 b) behavioral, stimulus-response theory of learning.
 c) innate multilevel learning.　　 d) none of the above

2) Which of the following is NOT proposed by Renate Nummela Caine as part of her "Brain Learning Principles"?
 a) The brain is a nonparallel processor.　　 b) Learning engages the entire physiology.
 c) Emotions are critical to patterning.　　 d) The search for meaning through patterning.

3) Traditionally, schools have focused on which model?
 a) assessment/learning　　 b) instruction/teaching　　 c) teaching/learning

4) Schools began to attempt restructuring assessment design to foster relational understanding rather than instrumental understanding in what decade?
 a) 1920s　　　　 b) 1980s　　　　 c) 1960s　　　　 d) 1990s

5) Cognitive scientists agree that children actively "construct" knowledge based upon what they already know and by interacting with . . .
 a) their teachers.　　 b) their textbooks.　　 c) their environment.　　 d) their homework.

6) Authentic assessment focuses on _____ _____ with end products, performances, or presentations centered on real-world problems, current events, or issues at the heart of the field of study or discipline.

7) In authentic assessment, _____ are responsible for monitoring their own performance based upon the criteria for excellence.

8) In authentic assessment, the _____ contains what needs to be done to improve the performance next time.

9) Alternative assessment and authentic assessment are synonymous terms.　　 TRUE　 FALSE

10) Students automatically organize knowledge into mental pictures for retention.　 TRUE　 FALSE

Section Review Questions

11) The Teaching-Learning Cycle begins with the learner by informally assessing each individual's _____ _____ _____ _____, including common areas of misunderstandings.

12) Learners rarely achieve complex tasks without multiple trial runs.   TRUE   FALSE

13) Teachers can expect _____ scores and _____ performance if their assessment does not match instruction.

14) What seven principles consistent with authentic assessment can be used to guide instruction?
    a) _____
    b) _____
    c) _____
    d) _____
    e) _____
    f) _____
    g) _____

15) Rank the following in sequence (1-3) of occurrence within the Teaching-Learning Cycle.
    _____ Adjust instruction based upon the evidence from the assessment.
    _____ Plan what evidence will document achievement of the learning target.
    _____ Collect the evidence through assessment embedded within the instruction.

16) By focusing on the _____ _____ _____ and the evidence necessary to document progress toward those targets, learners and teachers are more likely to hit the targets.

17) Which of the following is NOT accurate in considering the design process of the Teaching-Learning Cycle?
    a) The design process should be attempted with a team of teachers.
    b) The authentic assessment is designed to document achievement of the targeted learning.
    c) The design process should be attempted by individual teachers in isolation.
    d) The authentic assessment should be embedded in a larger assessment system.

18) Once the assessment is designed, then teachers can move to _____ design.

19) Which of the following are teaching strategies that might support the learner in achieving the learning targets?
    a) scaffolding, or thinking out loud   b) direct instruction   c) cooperative groups
    d) mind maps and graphic organizers   e) all of the above

20) _____ are a personal way of sharing progress toward learning targets over time.

The Power of Student Portfolios

Focus on Student Portfolios

While research persuasively demonstrates the power of portfolios for measuring student performance, many traditional instructors have yet to embrace this tool for assessment. Your task in this exercise is to write a persuasive mini-essay, designed to encourage a traditional teacher to use portfolios in his or her classroom. Use the "Online Resources" links in the "Measuring Student Performance" section of the companion CD-ROM to build evidence for your argument. These links will reveal valuable information on portfolios. Your argument should:

    1) Define student portfolios.
    2) List and describe what portfolios should contain.
    3) State both positive and negative findings of several studies on the use of student portfolios.
    4) Summarize and conclude your argument.

Why Should You Consider Using Student Portfolios in your Classroom?

_____

_____

_____

_____

_____

_____

_____

_____

_____

_____

_____

_____

_____

_____

_____

_____

_____

Locating Exemplary Lesson Plans

Lesson Plans Online

Coming up with ideas for classroom activities can be a demanding and tiring proposition. Teachers are constantly challenged to motivate and educate their students through engaging and creative activities. As your teaching career progresses, you will create some solid winners and absolute "bombs" when it comes to activities. Fortunately, there are thousands of other teachers in the same situation. The World Wide Web holds a vast archive of many exemplary lesson plans. In fact, entire Web sites are devoted to gathering "best practices" of teachers everywhere. In this activity, you will locate three such model lesson plans and share them with a group of students in your class.

Directions:

1) Connect to an Internet search engine using the "Web Search Tools" list found on the "Interactive Web Exercises" section of the CD-ROM.
2) Type "lesson plans" in the search query field. Execute the search.
3) Follow the links produced by the search engine until you locate collections of lesson plans.
4) Complete the information in the sections below and on the following page.
5) Share your findings with a group of three fellow students in your class.
6) Pick your favorite lesson plan and summarize it in the section provided.

Lesson Plans Online

List the URL: http://_____

What is the title of the lesson plan?
_____

What age group(s), grade level(s), and subject area(s) does the lesson target ?
_____

What are the learning objectives of the lesson?
_____
_____

What materials or supplies are needed to deliver the lesson? Is it practical and reproducible?
_____
_____

Describe what you liked most about this particular lesson plan.
_____
_____
_____

Lesson Plans Online

List the URL: http://_____

What is the title of the lesson plan?

_____

What age group(s), grade level(s), and subject area(s) does the lesson target ?

_____

What are the learning objectives of the lesson?

_____

_____

What materials or supplies are needed to deliver the lesson? Is it practical and reproducible?

_____

_____

Describe what you liked most about this particular lesson plan.

_____

_____

_____

_____

Lesson Plans Online

List the URL: http://_____

What is the title of the lesson plan?

_____

What age group(s), grade level(s), and subject area(s) does the lesson target ?

_____

What are the learning objectives of the lesson?

_____

_____

What materials or supplies are needed to deliver the lesson? Is it practical and reproducible?

_____

_____

Describe what you liked most about this particular lesson plan.

_____

_____

_____

_____

Favorite Lesson Plan from Fellow Team Member

Lesson Plans Online

List the URL: http://_____

What is the title of the lesson plan?
_____

What age group(s), grade level(s), and subject area(s) does the lesson target ?
_____

What are the learning objectives of the lesson?
_____
_____

What materials or supplies are needed to deliver the lesson? Is it practical and reproducible?
_____
_____

Describe what you liked most about this particular lesson plan.
_____
_____
_____

Measuring Student Performance

Accountability and Lesson Planning

One of today's major educational buzzwords is "accountability." Accountability refers to the linking of funding for schools and teachers to objective indicators of student success. The most widely recognized indicators are the completion of programs (high school graduation), suitable employment after graduation, and rising scores on standardized examinations. To address this demand, many state departments of education have proposed a series of "educational standards" and "curriculum frameworks" — benchmarks for student performance in various subjects at various grade levels.

One of the best examples of statewide educational standards comes from Florida. The Sunshine State Standards identify what Florida public school students should know and be able to do in each of the academic areas at the end of each of four grade levels: Pre-K to 2nd grade, 3rd to 5th grades, 6th to 8th grades, and 9th to 12th grades. These standards describe student achievement for which the state will hold schools accountable. These Sunshine State Standards are categorized into the subject areas of language arts, mathematics, science, social studies, music, visual arts, theater, dance, health, physical education, and foreign languages. Below is an example.

Mathematics
Grades 3-5

Number Sense, Concepts, and Operations
Standard 1: The student understands the different ways numbers are represented and used in the real world.

1) Names whole numbers combining 3-digit numeration (hundreds, tens, ones) and the use of number periods, such as ones, thousands, and millions and associates verbal names, written word names, and standard numerals with whole numbers, commonly used fractions, decimals, and percents.
2) Understands the relative size of whole numbers, commonly used fractions, decimals, and percents.
3) Understands concrete and symbolic representations of whole numbers, fractions, decimals, and percents in real-world situations.
4) Understands that numbers can be represented in a variety of equivalent forms using whole numbers, decimals, fractions, and percents .

In the following exercise, you will build a lesson plan around one of the "objective performance indicators" found among the federal and state educational standards. The "Online Resources" of the "Measuring Student Performance" section of the CD-ROM offers links to "Goals 2000" (the U.S. Department of Education's key document on educational standards) and to exemplary sets of state standards (California's "Challenge Standards" and Florida's "Sunshine State Standards"). Also, the "Developing Educational Standards" link provides a state-by-state look at standards and accountability.

Measuring Student Performance

Accountability and Lesson Planning

In this activity, you will create a lesson plan that is aligned with a specific educational standard for a given subject and grade level. These standards can be found in the sets of state standards listed in the "Online Resources" of the "Measuring Student Performance" section of the CD-ROM. Direct links are provided to California's "Challenge Standards" and Florida's "Sunshine State Standards." Use the "Developing Educational Standards" link if you wish to investigate other states' standards.

Build your lesson plan using the "Micro-Teach" model described in the "Lesson Plan Format for Micro-Teach: A Step-by-Step Guide" article found on the CD-ROM. Be sure to reflect the specific educational standard you have selected in your lesson plan.

PREPLANNING
STEP ONE: Select a specific educational standard for a specific topic and grade level.
STEP TWO: Plan a creative learning activity to teach this educational standard, addressing each section of the "Micro-Teach" lesson plan model:
1) **Describe the rationale of this lesson.** 2) **Describe the learning goals/outcomes of this lesson.**
3) **Describe the set/springboard for this lesson.** 4) **Enter the topic outline for this lesson.**
5) **Describe the teacher activities required for this lesson.** 6) **Describe student participation.**
7) **Offer higher-level/critical thinking questions for this lesson.** 8) **Write a closure narrative.**
9) **Describe the materials/resources required.** 10) **Describe the evaluation/assessment methods.**

BUILDING THE LESSON PLAN DIRECTIONS

STEP ONE:
Launch your Web browser.
Insert the *Technology for Teachers* CD-ROM.
Open the "index.htm" file on the CD.
Click the "Interactive Web Exercises" icon.
Click "Micro-Teach Lesson Plan Exercise."

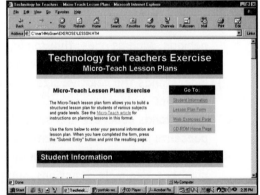

STEP TWO:
Type your lesson plan in the fields of the "Micro-Teach Lesson Plan" form. Do not forget to address a specific standard in the "goals/outcomes" and "evaluation/assessment" fields.

When you have completed the lesson plan, press the "Submit" button. This will create a copy of your lesson plan for printing. Place the printed copy in the portfolio workbook.

Measuring Student Performance

Structured Reflection Journal

Write several paragraphs on your thoughts and opinions regarding "Measuring Student Performance." Check with your instructor for the desired length of your response. Consider responding to:

* What are the benefits of authentic assessment? Why is authentic assessment going to be difficult to explain to parents, the public, and the media?

* What are several key principles in designing authentic assessment? Why are these important?

* Compare authentic assessment to traditional assessment. Discuss the importance of standards.

* What are several differences between professional portfolios and classroom portfolios? What role does a "rubric" play in portfolio design?

JOURNAL INSTRUCTIONS

STEP ONE:
1) Insert the *Technology for Teachers* CD-ROM.
2) If the CD-ROM does not auto-load, launch your Web browser and open the "index.htm" file on the CD-ROM. This file can be found in the ROOT folder of the CD-ROM. (That's the first folder that opens when you double click on the icon to look at your CD-ROM drive contents.) This page will load in your browser.
3) Click the "Measuring Student Performance" icon.
4) Scroll to the "Interactive Exercises" section of this page and click the desired question under "Structured Journal Exercises."

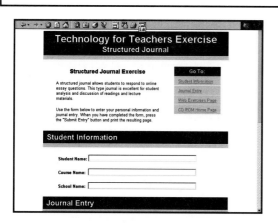

STEP TWO:
Click in each field of the "Structured Journal" form and enter the following:

1) Type your name (first name, then last).
2) Type the name of this course.
3) Type the name of your school or college.
4) Type your journal entry in the "Comments" field. Entries can be up to 20 pages of text in length and can be copied and pasted to the form from a word processor. Remember to place a "double-spaced" return between paragraphs.

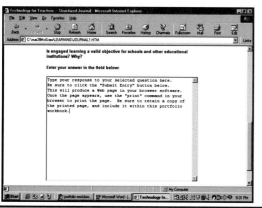

STEP THREE: Submit Entry

Click the button located at the bottom of the form. This will produce a Web page in your browser with your comments. Click the "Print" button in your browser. This will print your journal entry.

Place this journal entry inside the portfolio workbook to complete the assignment. Your instructor will give you due dates for each activity.

Open Reflection Journal

Questions for Reflection Journals

The purpose of the "open reflection" exercise is to encourage you to document your insights and questions about this topic. This record of your thoughts can serve as a "springboard" for reflective thinking—the beginning of an "internal dialogue" with your own thoughts as you gain more knowledge and experience. While this exercise is truly open-ended (that is, you can enter any comment you desire), consider writing about broad questions like the following:

- What is the most important lesson you have learned in this section? Why?
- What are your personal strengths and weaknesses in this area?
- How would you implement what you have learned about this topic in a classroom? What specific strategies would you use? What type of lesson plans would you develop?
- What is the greatest obstacle for using this type of technology in traditional classrooms?
- What questions remain unanswered about this topic?

JOURNAL INSTRUCTIONS
STEP ONE:
From the CD-ROM home page, select the "Measuring Student Performance" icon. Next, scroll down to the "Interactive Web Exercises" section and click the "Reflection Journal" option.

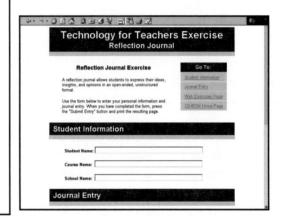

STEP TWO:

Click in each field on the form that appears, and type the following:

Type in your name and the name of your course and school. In the "Entry Title" field, type a meaningful title for your entry. Click in the comment field directly below and begin typing your journal entry. Remember, you can write your reflection in a word processing program, run spelling and grammar checking, and "cut-and-paste" your work into the comment field.

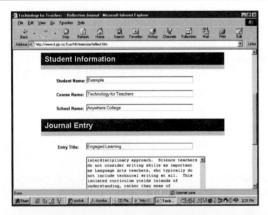

STEP THREE:
Click the button located at the bottom of the form. This will produce a Web page in your browser with your comments. Click the "Print" button in your browser. This will print your journal entry.

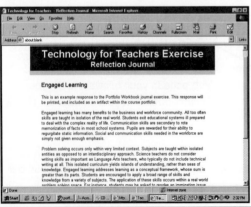

Place this journal entry inside the portfolio workbook to complete the assignment. Your instructor will give you due dates for each activity.

Instructional Uses of the Internet

Perhaps the greatest unrealized technology resource for instructors is the Internet—in particular, the multimedia environment of the World Wide Web. The relative ease of use, quick accessibility, and growing interactivity of the Web makes it a perfect agent for enhancing and expanding instructional practices—both for traditional classroom and distance learners alike. Along with the challenge of providing Internet access for every student, educators also face the task of harnessing this resource to further instructional goals and purposes—to rethink the acts of teaching and learning and the place of this technology tool in the process.

To introduce the "Instructional Uses of the Internet," the *Technology for Teachers* CD-ROM includes the following materials:

"Instruction and the Internet: A Survey of the Best Strategies" describes a dozen ways in which K-12 instructors across America are integrating Internet resources into traditional instruction. "Hot links" to example sites show these strategies "in action."

"Companion Web Sites: Extending Traditional Classrooms with Web Resources" proposes simple guidelines for the creation and maintenance of Web sites to support and supplement traditional classroom courses.

To access these materials, load the CD-ROM, select the "Instructional Uses of the Internet" icon, and click the desired article title.

In addition, this portfolio workbook contains the following learning activities:

> **Review Questions: Instructional Uses of the Internet**
> **15 Terms Every Teacher Should Know**
> **Online Activity: Locating Educational Web Sites**
> **Online Activity: Evaluating Educational Web Sites**
> **Research Assignment: Researching your District's Internet Policy**
> **Online Activity: Creating a Basic Web Page**
> **Online Activity: Creating a Personal Web Page**
> **"Hands-On" Activity: Building a Virtual Library**
> **"Hands-On" Activity: Creating a Companion Web Site**
> **Structured Reflection Journal**
> **Open Reflection Journal**

Instructional Uses of the Internet

The Internet is opening a world of new learning opportunities. The vast resources of the Internet—especially the World Wide Web—hold enormous potential for educational purposes. Teachers must learn to harness this resource. Internet resources will soon become one of the "normal tools" of every classroom.

SECTIONS:

* **Instruction and the Internet**
* **Companion Web Sites**

Section Review Questions

1) At the heart of all good instruction lie the two basic qualities of . . .
    a) communication and evaluation.
    b) communication and interaction.
    c) evaluation and reflection.
    d) reflection and communication.

2) The World Wide Web extends research capabilities of traditional research with . . .
    a) additional content.
    b) multimedia.
    c) a variety of search engines.
    d) all of the above.

3) Instructor-created Web pages containing links to Internet sites pertinent to the subject matter of the instructor's course are called . . .
    a) search engines.
    b) virtual libraries.
    c) content filters.
    d) link lists.

4) Which of the following is NOT an advantage of "Web-publishing"?
    a) lower cost
    b) reaches larger audiences
    c) content filters
    d) easy-to-use publishing tools

5) Online discussion that is live, instantaneous, and immediately interactive is termed . . .
    a) synchronous.
    b) parallel.
    c) asynchronous.
    d) nonparallel.

6) The _____ _____ allows students to communicate either through "real-time" chat or, more often, via electronic mail with experts on given topics.

7) Online drill and practice should be used to _____ previously learned information, never to introduce new information.

8) The best virtual field trips allow _____ _____ for "closer looks" and deeper details for student investigation.

9) Virtual museums are well suited for educational "repurposing."   TRUE FALSE

10) Many online news sites provide instant access to news stories and often a deeper analysis of news coverage than television broadcast network news.   TRUE FALSE

15 Terms Nobody Wants to Memorize, but Every Teacher Should Know

1) cyberspace:

_____

_____

2) virtual libraries:

_____

_____

3) keyword search:

_____

_____

4) mega-list search:

_____

_____

5) electronic publishing:

_____

_____

6) virtual discussion groups:

_____

_____

7) asynchronous communication:

_____

_____

8) expert forum:

_____

_____

9) virtual field trips:

_____

_____

10) online exam:

_____

11) virtual survey:

_____

_____

12) companion Web site:

_____

_____

13) syllabus page:

_____

14) threaded discussion group:

_____

_____

15) self-grading quizzes:

_____

Locating Educational Web Sites

Lesson plans are not the only instructional resource on the Internet. There are literally thousands of Web sites that can be used with students in many other ways. The Internet is fast becoming as valuable as the standard textbook for instruction. Some would argue that educational Web sites have distinct advantages over textbooks. Web sites can be readily updated to include the latest news and information. Web sites can also be more interactive and engaging than textbooks. Entire sites can contain complex detail on only one topic, while others present a broad range of related topics.

Locating an educational Web site is not a difficult task. There are two primary approaches for locating educational Web sites.

Locating Web Sites with Search Engines

Standard queries with Internet search engines, such as Altavista, Excite, or Yahoo!, will yield many links to educational Web sites. Search engines themselves often contain link listings by topic with dedicated resources for K-12 teachers. Of special interest is the "Lycos Top 5% of Educational Web Sites." Visit this list at www.lycos.com.

Lycos' Top 5% of Educational Web Sites

Locating Web Sites with Mega-Lists

Many educators and related professionals have spent large amounts of time locating sites and creating lists of resources. These lists of educational Web sites are organized by subject matter, grade level, and even topic. Keep in mind that while such sites can be time saving, none are completely comprehensive. A great example of a mega-list of educational Web sites is the Florida Information Resources Network (FIRN) "Instructional Resources" list. This site is maintained by the Florida Department of Education at www.firn.edu.

Florida's FIRN K-12 Educational Mega-list

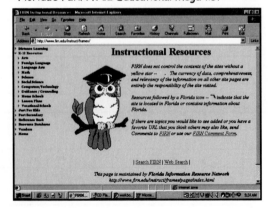

LOCATE AN EDUCATIONAL WEB SITE

Use the resources above, or your preferred Internet search method, to locate an educational K-12 Web site. List the URL below. On the next page, you will evaluate this Web site.

URL: http://_____

Instructional Uses of the Internet

Evaluating Educational Web Sites

Educational Web Sites

Your quest to locate educational K-12 Web sites has most likely uncovered a large number of sites. As with instructional software, educators must review and evaluate Web sites before using them in classroom settings. You may find sites that are well designed at first look, but under closer scrutiny fail to live up to their promises. Some sites may even have information that is inappropriate for young learners.

It is the educator's responsibility to evaluate Web sites for appropriate content and educational value. Your school district, state education office, or private school may provide guidelines and requirements to follow before using Web-based materials for instruction. Check with your college or local school district for policies in your area.

Use the Web site you located on the previous page for the following activity.

ACTIVITY INSTRUCTIONS

STEP ONE:
Launch your Web browser.
Insert the *Technology for Teachers* CD-ROM.
Open the "index.htm" file on the CD.
Click the "Interactive Web Exercises" icon.

STEP TWO:

Select the "Web Site Evaluation" option.

Click each field on the form that appears and type the appropriate information.

Click the checkboxes and radio buttons (empty circles) to record your evaluation of the Web site.

Summarize your thoughts and comments about the site in the "Comment" field at the bottom of the form.

STEP THREE:

Click the button located at the bottom of the form.
This will produce a Web page in your browser with your comments. Click the "Print" button in your browser to print your journal entry.

Place this journal entry inside the portfolio workbook to complete the assignment. Your instructor will give you due dates for each activity.

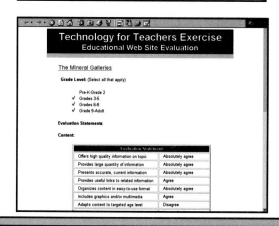

Instructional Uses of the Internet

Researching Your District's Internet Policy

Educational Web Sites

There is a great debate over the freedom of information versus censorship. The Internet complicates this issue exponentially. While we strive to provide all students with equal access to information, we must protect them from inappropriate content. Pornography, political extremism, and access to firearms and nonprescription drugs are only a few areas of potential danger for students accessing an unrestricted Internet. Software such as content filters and firewalls can attempt to block out content of this nature. But is this the best approach? A student seeking to write a report on breast cancer would find many potential resources of information unavailable where such filters and firewalls are used.

Should students have unrestricted access to the Internet? Should schools and school systems be held liable for damages resulting from access to inappropriate content? In this exercise you will locate and debate the Internet access policy of your local school district or institution.

ACTIVITY INSTRUCTIONS

STEP ONE:

Contact your local school district office or appropriate agency governing the operation of schools within your area. Try looking at your local district's Web site.

Request a copy of their Internet access policy, or Web policy guidelines. If your area does not have such a document, contact a local school. Many schools have individual policies and procedures for Internet access for students. Obtain one of these from the school administration.

Review the document carefully. As you read, consider the following:
> What indicators of censorship are evident?
> Are there appropriate permissions from parents?
> Is the policy too restrictive?
> What software or other technical solutions have been implemented
> to protect students while allowing sufficient access?

STEP TWO:

Answer each of the questions on the following page.

Internet Policy Review

1) Where did you obtain the Internet policy and who was your contact?

_____

2) Does this policy pertain to an individual school or an entire district?

_____

3) List at least four strengths of this policy.

    a) _____

       _____

    b) _____

       _____

    c) _____

       _____

    d) _____

       _____

4) List at least four weaknesses of this policy.

    a) _____

       _____

    b) _____

       _____

    c) _____

       _____

    d) _____

       _____

5) What type of problems is this policy creating for teachers and students?

_____

_____

6) Do you agree with this policy? Why or why not?

_____

_____

_____

7) What would you do to improve it?

_____

_____

_____

_____

_____

_____

_____

Instructional Uses of the Internet

Creating a Basic Web Page

Creating a basic Web page is not the complex proposition it once was. Until just
a few years ago, Web authors had to learn a scripting language known as HTML, or
Hypertext Markup Language. While this language was very simple in comparison to other
computer programming languages, it was not as friendly as the graphic interfaces to which the vast
majority of computer users had become accustomed. Simple HTML editors were followed by a family
of software tools referred to as WYSIWYG (What You See is What You Get) editors. These software
applications generate Web pages through a graphic user interface and control icons. Adobe PageMill
and Microsoft Front Page are two of the best-known tools in this category. The first Web page
construction activity featured on the *Technology for Teachers* CD-ROM allows you to experiment with
simple HTML syntax. Follow the directions below for a "hands-on" HTML experience.

PRACTICE BUILDING HTML CODE

STEP ONE:

Launch your Web browser.
Insert the *Technology for Teachers* CD-ROM.
Open the "index.htm" file on the CD.
Click the "Interactive Web Exercises" icon.
Click the "HTML Demonstration" option.

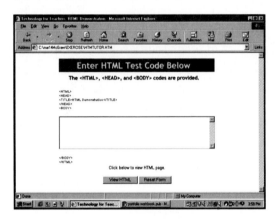

STEP TWO:

To learn more about HTML code, follow the "Online
Resources" links on the CD-ROM in this topic's section.
"A Beginner's Guide to HTML" from the National Center
for Supercomputing Applications and the "HTML Quick
Reference" from Tulane University are great places to
begin. Several more detailed treatments of HTML
coding and Web page construction are provided among
the online links.

STEP THREE:

Practice building simple HTML pages using the "HTML Test Code" form. Type in the desired text and
HTML tags (as explained in the resources in step 2) and click the "View HTML" button. Your Web
browser will open a new window and display the formatted HTML text.

Experiment with some of the most basic HTML tags: <B> Bold, <I> Italics, <U> Underline, <CENTER>
Center, <HR> Horizontal line, <P> Paragraph break,
 Line break, etc.

Instructional Uses of the Internet

Creating a Personal Web Page

Thousands of individuals have created personal Web pages. These pages often introduce the individual by describing their academic background, job history, and special skills and accomplishments. Contact information is also frequently included. In this activity, you will create a simple personal Web page using an interactive form on the CD-ROM.

In order for others to visit this page, you must "post" it to the Internet. To do so, you must have access to a Web server connected to the Internet. If you already subscribe to an Internet provider, contact them regarding procedures for posting personal Web pages. Many providers offer free space for the posting of personal pages with your paid subscription to their services. Check with your instructor on policies and procedures for similar Web posting and publishing resources provided by your college or educational institution.

ACTIVITY INSTRUCTIONS

STEP ONE:

Launch your Web browser.
Insert the *Technology for Teachers* CD-ROM.
Open the "index.htm" file on the CD.
Click the "Interactive Web Exercises" icon.
Click "Student Web Page Exercise."

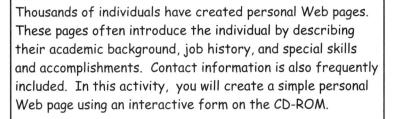

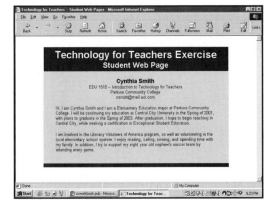

STEP TWO:

Click each field on the form that appears and type the appropriate information.

Type at least two paragraphs about yourself in the form. (Double-space between each paragraph.) In the first paragraph describe your academic career (your major, your continued educational plans, and your long-range vocational goals). In the second paragraph, enter any personal information (hobbies, involvement in clubs and service agencies, etc.).

Click the "Submit Entry" button to build the Web page.

Print your page and include it in the portfolio workbook.

Building a Virtual Library

CREATE YOUR OWN VIRTUAL LIBRARY

One way to maximize your students' "Web surfing" experience is to create a list of links specifically for your course. In this project you will create such a list—your own "virtual library." In this exercise, you will plan a virtual library of resources, gathering all the information necessary to build a Web page from these links. Follow the steps below to start your project.

STEP ONE: Select a topic or subject area.
Before you begin your virtual library, you must select the subject matter or specific topic for your collection. Some examples might contain links to famous figures of the 1920s, math activities for 5th graders, endangered species, literary critiques of early American authors, news sites with archives, women in history, aviation engineering, online lesson plans for elementary educators, online educational games for children, etc. Note that these examples range from very broad to quite specific. Try to pick a topic or subject you will use in the future.

STEP TWO: Search for Web sites. Review Web sites.
Use popular Internet search engines to locate sites relevant to your topic and/or subject. Follow the links the search engine generates. Evaluate the site as to whether or not you think others would benefit from the information there. Use whatever criteria you wish to compare sites. When you locate a site you wish to be a part of your virtual library, be sure to record the URL (Web address).

Try one of the following search engines or use one listed in the "Web Search Tools" found in the "Interactive Web Exercises" section of the CD-ROM.

ALTAVISTA   at http://www.altavista.com
YAHOO!   at http://www.yahoo.com
EXCITE   at http://www.excite.com
HOTBOT   at http://www.hotbot.com

STEP THREE: Add the selected site to your library list.
Use the following page in the portfolio workbook to add each site to your virtual library list. Be sure to write a brief description of the site, including the type and nature of information available at that site.

OPTIONAL STEP FOUR: Create the list as a Web page.
Check with your instructor for available software that you can use to actually create your virtual library as a Web page. You can use simple HTML if you know how. Many free tools are available for Web page authoring, such as Netscape Communicator's Composer or Microsoft's FrontPage Express (a component of Internet Explorer). Include the completed page within this portfolio.

Virtual Library Project

Student Name_____ Course Number and Section _____

Date ____ / ____ / ____   Search Engines Used _____

Subject or Topic of Virtual Library: _____

Link List

1) **Title**_____
   URL: http://_____
   Description: _____
   _____
   _____

2) **Title**_____
   URL: http://_____
   Description: _____
   _____
   _____

3) **Title**_____
   URL: http://_____
   description: _____
   _____
   _____

4) **Title**_____
   URL: http://_____
   Description: _____
   _____
   _____

5) **Title**_____
   URL: http://_____
   Description: _____
   _____
   _____

Continue to Next Page

Virtual Library Project: Page Two

Link List Continued;

6) Title_____

   URL: http://_____

   Description: _____

   _____

   _____

7) Title_____

   URL: http://_____

   Description: _____

   _____

   _____

8) Title_____

   URL: http://_____

   Description: _____

   _____

   _____

9) Title_____

   URL: http://_____

   Description: _____

   _____

   _____

10) Title_____

   URL: http://_____

   Description: _____

   _____

   _____

SITE RANKING: Rank the sites you have selected in order of importance, relevance, and value. Your ranking should reflect each site's value to students or potential visitors to your list.

1 _____   6 _____

2 _____   7 _____

3 _____   8 _____

4 _____   9 _____

5 _____   10 _____

Instructional Uses of the Internet

Creating a Companion Web Site

A companion Web site is a collection of Web pages designed to support and supplement the instructional activities of traditional classroom courses. A companion Web site is not a distance learning course that seeks to replace traditional instruction; rather, a companion Web site is a "Web presence" for a traditional course—a different, more convenient "point of access" for course materials, assignments, and information. A companion Web site can be no more than an online syllabus and class calendar or it can expand to a highly interactive environment with online discussion groups, interactive quizzes, student journals, and much, much more. Read more about these Web sites in the "Companion Web Sites: Extending Traditional Classrooms with Web Resources" article in the "Instructional Uses of the Internet" section of the CD-ROM.

Companion Web sites are designed to both enhance and extend traditional classroom instruction. The companion Web site enhances traditional learning by providing easier and broader access to existing course materials—syllabi, outlines, lecture notes, handouts, assignments, and special announcements. Likewise, the companion Web site extends traditional learning by opening the possibilities of online interactive exercises—multimedia "lectures," self-grading quizzes, online student journals and portfolios, real-time "chat," and threaded discussion groups.

Designing a Companion Web Site

All the pages of a companion Web site should be built around a common layout and graphical "look and feel." Consistent design is the key to efficient and effective delivery of Web-based information. The best companion Web sites are built around a single design template with limited, tasteful graphics and clear navigational controls.

The simplest companion Web site consists of three foundation pages: (1) the **welcome page**, (2) the **course description page**, and (3) the **contact page**. The welcome page usually contains a short greeting and a brief description of the course. This page serves as the "table of contents" for all other pages. The course description page reproduces a Web version of the course syllabus and outline. The contact page provides a simple Web form for sending electronic mail to the instructor.

Using Templates to Build a Companion Web Site

In this exercise, you will use the templates on the following pages to build a storyboard of a companion Web site to support a course you teach or plan to teach. Specific directions for constructing welcome, course description, and contact pages are found on the templates. Place a copy of these storyboard pages in the portfolio workbook.

If possible, use "visual" Web page construction software to build actual Web pages from the storyboards. Netscape Composer and Microsoft FrontPage Express are free, easy-to-use Web-building tools included with the Netscape Navigator and Microsoft Internet Explorer Web browsers. Either of these tools would be perfect for building these simple Web pages.

Companion Web Site Storyboard

COURSE WELCOME PAGE

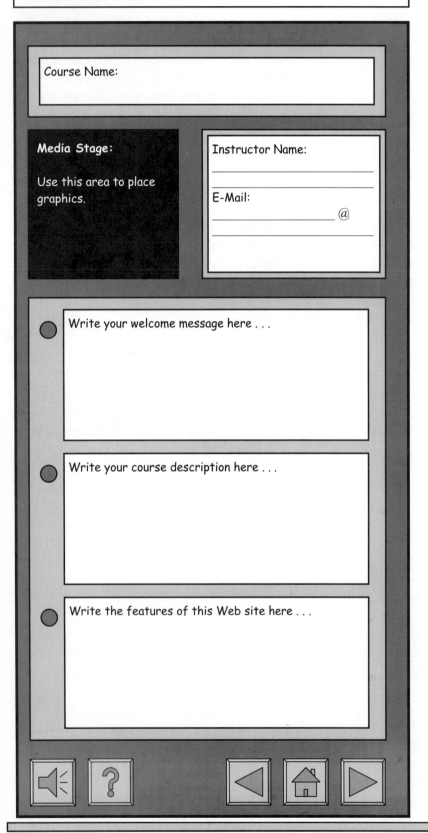

Course Name:

Media Stage:

Use this area to place graphics.

Instructor Name:
_____

E-Mail:
_____ @

Write your welcome message here . . .

Write your course description here . . .

Write the features of this Web site here . . .

As Web sites become more complex, creating storyboards to plan them is becoming a more common practice. The next few pages provide you with templates you can use with students to make a blueprint for a potential Web site.

The welcome message should consist of a single sentence greeting visitors to your Web site.

The course description should be a brief paragraph summarizing the topics covered in this course.

The Web features section should list any special resources found at this Web site.

Companion Web Site Storyboard

COURSE DESCRIPTION PAGE

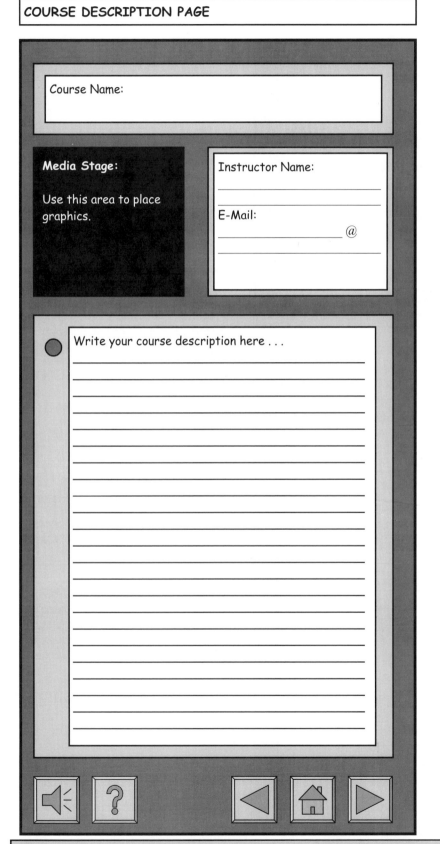

Course Name:

Media Stage:

Use this area to place graphics.

Instructor Name:
_____
_____

E-Mail:
_____ @
_____

Write your course description here . . .

The course description should consist of a brief description of the course's subject matter, textbook and course materials information, a calendar of events, special announcements, and assignments and grading criteria .

Companion Web Site Storyboard

COURSE CONTACT PAGE

Course Name:

Media Stage:

Use this area to insert the teacher's photo.

Instructor Name:
_____

E-Mail:
_____ @

○ **Phone:**

Enter your work phone number including area code.

○ **Fax:**

Enter your work fax number including area code.

○ **Full Mailing Address:**

Enter your full work mailing address including your office or classroom location.

○ **Schedule of Classes:**

Enter your schedule of classes indicating any planning or "free" periods.

Instructional Uses of the Internet

Structured Reflection Journal

Write several paragraphs on your thoughts and opinions regarding "Instructional Uses of the Internet." Check with your instructor for the desired length of your response. Consider responding to:

* What are some of the potential benefits of using Internet resources in the classrooms? What might be some of the challenges?

* An increasing number of Internet sites are inappropriate for children. What strategies might teachers use to minimize the danger of students accessing such sites?

* List and describe several virtual libraries.

* As a teacher, how might you use an expert forum? Give a specific example of this within a subject area you are currently teaching or would like to teach.

JOURNAL INSTRUCTIONS

STEP ONE:
1) Insert the *Technology for Teachers* CD-ROM.
2) If the CD-ROM does not auto-load, launch your Web browser and open the "index.htm" file on the CD-ROM. This file can be found in the ROOT folder of the CD-ROM. (That's the first folder that opens when you double click on the icon to look at your CD-ROM drive contents.) This page will load in your browser.
3) Click the "Instructional Uses of the Internet" icon.
4) Scroll to the "Interactive Exercises" section of this page and click the desired question under "Structured Journal Exercises.".

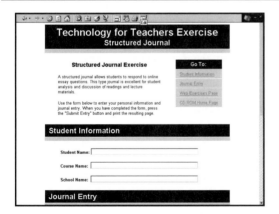

STEP TWO:
Click in each field of the "Structured Journal" form and enter the following:

1) Type your name (first name, then last).
2) Type the name of this course.
3) Type the name of your school or college.
4) Type your journal entry in the "Comments" field. Entries can be up to 20 pages of text in length and can be copied and pasted to the form from a word processor. Remember to place a "double-spaced" return between paragraphs.

STEP THREE: Submit Entry

Click the button located at the bottom of the form.
This will produce a Web page in your browser with your comments. Click the "Print" button in your browser. This will print your journal entry.

Place this journal entry inside the portfolio workbook to complete the assignment. Your instructor will give you due dates for each activity.

Instructional Uses of the Internet

Open Reflection Journal

Questions for Reflection Journals

The purpose of the "open reflection" exercise is to encourage you to document your insights and questions about this topic. This record of your thoughts can serve as a "springboard" for reflective thinking—the beginning of an "internal dialogue" with your own thoughts as you gain more knowledge and experience. While this exercise is truly open-ended (that is, you can enter any comment you desire), consider writing about broad questions like the following:

- What is the most important lesson you have learned in this section? Why?
- What are your personal strengths and weaknesses in this area?
- How would you implement what you have learned about this topic in a classroom? What specific strategies would you use? What type of lesson plans would you develop?
- What is the greatest obstacle for using this type of technology in traditional classrooms?
- What questions remain unanswered about this topic?

JOURNAL INSTRUCTIONS
STEP ONE:
From the CD-ROM home page, select the "Instructional Uses of the Internet" icon. Next, scroll down to the "Interactive Web Exercises" section and click the "Reflection Journal" option.

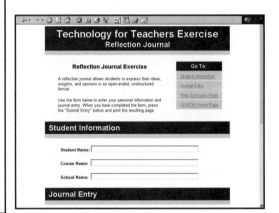

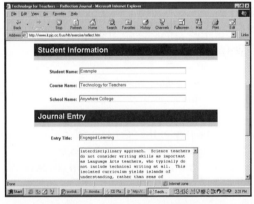

STEP TWO:

Click in each field on the form that appears, and type the following:

Type in your name and the name of your course and school. In the "Entry Title" field, type a meaningful title for your entry. Click in the comment field directly below and begin typing your journal entry. Remember, you can write your reflection in a word processing program, run spelling and grammar checking, and "cut-and-paste" your work into the comment field.

STEP THREE:

Click the button located at the bottom of the form. This will produce a Web page in your browser with your comments. Click the "Print" button in your browser. This will print your journal entry.

Place this journal entry inside the portfolio workbook to complete the assignment. Your instructor will give you due dates for each activity.

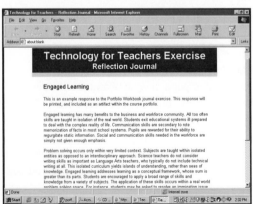

Appendix I:
Installing Additional Software Tools

Loading the CD-ROM

The *Technology for Teachers* CD-ROM is a "dual platform" tool, designed to work in both the Windows and Macintosh environments. The CD-ROM requires Windows 95, 98, or higher or Macintosh System 7.5 or higher. A fourth generation Web browser (Netscape Navigator 4.0 or Internet Explorer 4.0) or higher is required for the interactive Web exercises found on the CD-ROM. Microsoft's Internet Explorer is included on the CD-ROM if you do not have browser software.

Windows 95/98/2000

There are two ways to load the *Technology for Teachers* CD-ROM in the Windows environment.

First, you can load your Web browser and use the "FILE-OPEN" option. Browse to the CD-ROM and load the "index.htm" file in the CD-ROM root folder.

Second, you can run the Windows "install" program. Load this file by clicking the "START" button and choosing the "RUN" option. Browse for the CD-ROM and select the "install.exe" file. Click the "OK" button and this window will appear.

Choose "Install the CD-ROM startup icon" and press the "INSTALL" button. This will place a "Technology for Teachers" option in the "START-PROGRAMS" menu.

Macintosh

To load the *Technology for Teachers* CD-ROM in the Macintosh environment, insert the CD-ROM and the "T4TCDROM" icon will appear on the Desktop.

Double click this icon to display the files in the root folder of the CD-ROM. Scroll to the "INDEX.HTM" file. Double click this filename. This will automatically load your Web browser and display the CD-ROM "home" page.

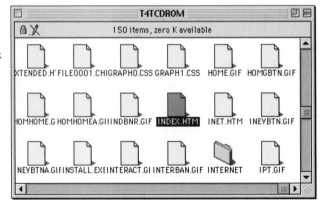

If you do not have a Web browser loaded on your computer, follow the instructions below to install Microsoft's Internet Explorer.

Microsoft Internet Explorer Installation

Microsoft's Internet Explorer for both the Windows and Mac platforms is included on the CD-ROM. To install the Windows version, run the Windows "install" program as described above. To install the Mac version, insert the CD-ROM and double click the "T4TCDROM" icon that appears on the Desktop. From the resulting file list, select the "MAC" folder and then the "IEXPLORE" folder. Finally, run the "IE5SETUP.EXE" program.

The installation procedure for Internet Explorer is the same for the Windows and Macintosh environments.

Once the install program is loaded, Internet Explorer displays a "Welcome" screen. Internet Explorer presents the license agreement in a scrolling window. Read this agreement carefully and click the "I accept" radio button and then the "NEXT" button.

NOTE: Internet Explorer is free software, provided at no charge by the Microsoft Corporation.

Next, select the desired "Installation Option." The "Install Now – Typical set of components" option installs the Web browser and a set of add-ons and multimedia enhancements. The "Install Minimal – or customize your browser" option allows you to select only the components you want and the folder in which to install them. The following directions apply to the "Install Now – Typical set of components" option.

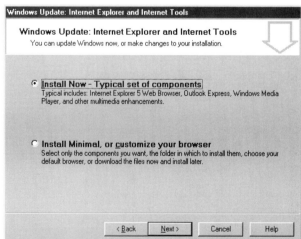

Microsoft Internet Explorer Installation (continued)

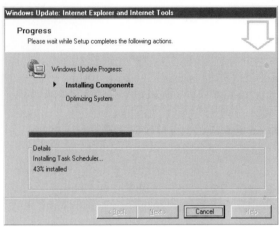

Once these decisions have been made, Internet Explorer will begin installation. This can be a lengthy process depending on the speed of your computer. You will be prompted to restart your computer before the installation is complete.

Adobe Acrobat Installation

Many of the articles on the CD-ROM appear in the Adobe Acrobat format. To view these files you need to install the Adobe Acrobat Reader.

To install the Windows version, run the Windows "install" program as described above. To install the Mac version, insert the CD-ROM and double click the "T4TCDROM" icon that appears on the desktop. From the resulting file list, select the "MAC" folder and then the "ACROBAT" folder. Finally, run the "AR40ENG2.EXE" program.

The installation procedure for Adobe Acrobat Reader is the same for the Windows and Macintosh environments.

Once the install program is loaded, the Adobe Acrobat Reader will copy several files to your computer to begin the installation process.

A "Welcome" screen begins the installation process. Read this page carefully and then press the "NEXT" button.

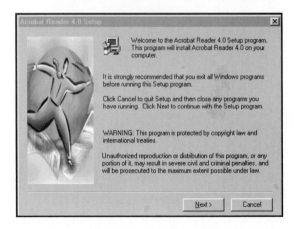

Adobe Acrobat Installation (continued)

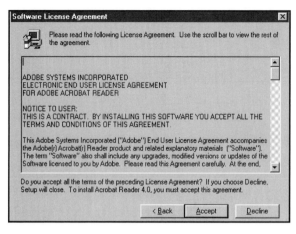

Next, the Adobe Acrobat Reader prompts you to agree with the Adobe licensing agreement. Read this agreement carefully and click "Accept."

NOTE: The Adobe Acrobat Reader is free software, provided at no charge by the Adobe Corporation.

Next, you need to select the "Destination Location" for the installation. To accept the default location, simply press the "NEXT" button. To change this location, use the "BROWSE" button.

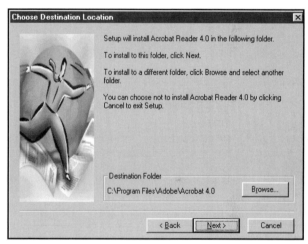

Once these decisions have been made, the Adobe Acrobat Reader will be installed. When the installation is complete, this final screen will appear.

Appendix II:

Answer Key for Section Review Questions and Key Article Quizzes

Section Review Questions Answer Key

On the following pages you will find the answers to each of the "Section Review Questions." The name of the article containing the answer is also listed for your convenience.

Promoting Engaged Learning	
Answer	Article Location
1. c) extended learning environments	The Evolving Classroom
2. c) very time-consuming	The Evolving Classroom
3. b) enhanced learning	The Evolving Classroom
4. student –centered	Old Story-New Story
5. educational staff	Old Story-New Story
6. learner outcomes	Old Story-New Story
7. learning styles	Learning Styles
8. Learning Styles Inventory	Learning Styles
9. TRUE	Learning Styles
10. TRUE	Basic Computing Concepts
Multimedia Student Authoring	
Answer	Article Location
1. c) taste	Elements of Multimedia
2. b) raster images	Elements of Multimedia
3. d) LRC	Elements of Multimedia
4. b) bandwidth	Elements of Multimedia
5. "fair use"	Elements of Multimedia
6. right	Harvesting the Web
7. multimedia authoring	Multimedia Student Authoring
8. periodic standard exams	Multimedia Student Authoring
9. TRUE	Multimedia Student Authoring
10. TRUE	Multimedia Student Authoring

Evaluating Instructional Software	
Answer	Article Location
1. d) emulation software	Building Blocks of CAI
2. d) offering initial training	Building Blocks of CAI
3. a) transfer of information	Building Blocks of CAI
4. b) discrimination	Building Blocks of CAI
5. optional choices	Building Blocks of CAI
6. recognition	Building Blocks of CAI
7. interaction	Building Blocks of CAI
8. large	Building Blocks of CAI
9. TRUE	Evaluating Educational Software
10. TRUE	Evaluating Educational Web Sites
Classroom Management Strategies	
Answer	Article Location
1. d) at the teacher's desk	Classroom Management Design
2. b) workstation rotation environments	Classroom Management Design
3. d) Such environments take the teacher less time to design . . .	Classroom Management Design
4. a) resource design	Classroom Management Design
5. computer labs	Classroom Management Design
6. diversified	Classroom Management Design
7. purposed areas	Classroom Management Design
8. learning objectives	Classroom Management Design
9. TRUE	Classroom Management Design
10. FALSE	Classroom Management Design

Section Review Questions Answer Key

Implementing Presentation Technologies	
Answer	Article Location
1. d) all of the above	Effective Classroom Presentations
2. c) selective attention	Effective Classroom Presentations
3. b) 3-5 pieces of information	Effective Classroom Presentations
4. b) every 2 minutes	Effective Classroom Presentations
5. d) templates	Effective Classroom Presentations
6. storyboarding	Effective Classroom Presentations
7. body and a conclusion	Effective Classroom Presentations
8. beginning	Effective Classroom Presentations
9. FALSE	Effective Classroom Presentations
10. FALSE	Effective Classroom Presentations
Measuring Student Performance	
Answer	Article Location
1. b) behavioral, stimulus-response theory of learning	Authentic Assessment
2. a) The brain is a nonparallel processor.	Authentic Assessment
3. b) instruction/teaching	Authentic Assessment
4. b) 1980s	Authentic Assessment
5. c) their environment	Authentic Assessment
6. engaged learning	Authentic Assessment
7. students	Authentic Assessment
8. feedback	Authentic Assessment
9. FALSE	Authentic Assessment
10. FALSE	Authentic Assessment

Section Review Questions Answer Key

Measuring Student Performance (continued)	
Answer	Article Location
11. understanding of targeted content	Authentic Assessment
12. TRUE	Authentic Assessment
13. low scores, poor performance	Authentic Assessment
14. 1) measure what it purports to measure, 2) align to agreed upon learning targets, 3) provide specific feedback for improvement 4) develop varying levels of thinking appropriately, 5) produce measurable, reliable evidence of achievement based upon clear criteria, 6) match the intended purpose, 7) be embedded with instruction	Authentic Assessment
15. 3, 1, 2	Authentic Assessment
16. intended learning targets	Authentic Assessment
17. c) The design process . . . attempted by individual teachers . . .	Authentic Assessment
18. instructional	Authentic Assessment
19. e) all of the above	Authentic Assessment
20. portfolios	Authentic Assessment
Instructional Uses of the Internet	
Answer	Article Location
1. b) communication and interaction	Instruction and the Internet
2. d) all of the above	Instruction and the Internet
3. b) virtual libraries	Instruction and the Internet
4. c) content filters	Instruction and the Internet
5. a) synchronous	Instruction and the Internet
6. expert forum	Instruction and the Internet
7. reinforce	Instruction and the Internet
8. optional navigation	Instruction and the Internet
9. TRUE	Instruction and the Internet
10. TRUE	Instruction and the Internet

1. D. transferring data from one computer to another	
2. B. a file	
3. C. prepare or initialize it for use	
4. A. a word processor	
5. D. a modem	
6. C. a database	
7. B. on disks (hard or floppy)	
8. B. the arrow keys	
9. C. a database	
10. B. publishing long text documents	
11. A. microprocessor (the CPU chip)	
12. D. a word processor	
13. C. describe the numerical data stored in the corresponding row or column	
14. B. a megabyte	
15. D. a port	
16. A. an operating system	
17. D. database manager	
18. B. a database manager	
19. A. the cursor	
20. A. an electronic spreadsheet	
21. D. Two files with the same name cannot exist in the same directory on the same disk	
22. C. record	
23. B. All hard disks are portable and transportable	
24. B. Information in RAM is lost when the computer is turned off	
25. C. word wrap	
26. A. the necessity of re-entering data	
27. C. a database manager	
28. C. 1000	

Evaluating Instructional Software Key Article Quiz Answers

1. FALSE	
2. D. simulations	
3. synthesis	
4. generalization	
5. discrimination	
6. TRUE	
7. recognition, recognition, recognition, recall, recall	
8. TRUE	
9. A. high quality feedback to student responses	
10. B. tutorials	
11. TRUE	
12. TRUE	
13. B. conditional branching	
14. A. hypertext	
15. C. educational games	
16. B. modules	
17. FALSE	
18. D. repetitive reinforcement of facts	
19. D. simulations	
20. D. simulations	
21. TRUE	
22. C. decision path	

Key Article Quiz Answer Key I

Implementing Presentation Technologies Key Article Quiz Answers

1. C. information chunking
2. C. hypertext arrangement of information and links
3. D. information chunking
4. TRUE
5. TRUE
6. B. 2
7. A. template that provides a framework of objects and colors
8. A. One
9. D. storyboard
10. D. summary slide
11. B. cognitive breaks
12. A. contrasting text and background colors
13. C. the ability to distinguish between characters in the chosen font face
14. C. font face
15. A. parallelism
16. TRUE
17. FALSE
18. TRUE
19. B. font substitution
20. FALSE
21. D. saturation color
22. FALSE
23. A. Bar graph
24. A. pie graph
25. TRUE

Appendix III:
Storyboard Templates

Multimedia Storyboard

Student Name: _____ Course # _____ Section #_____

TITLE SLIDE/PAGE

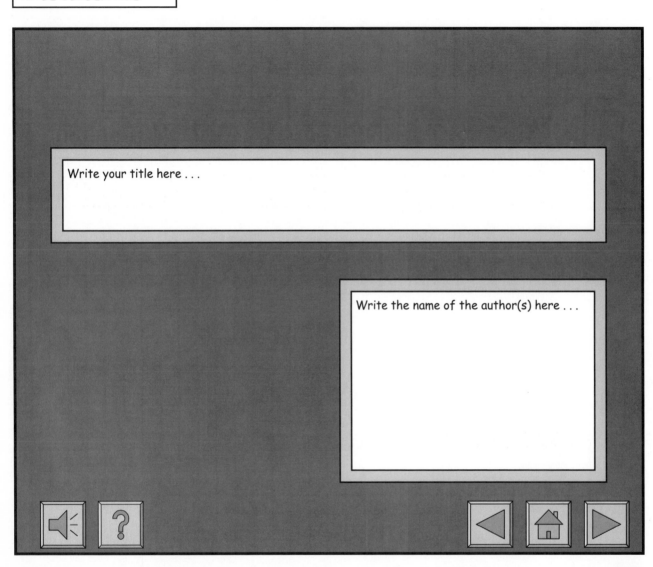

Write your title here . . .

Write the name of the author(s) here . . .

Media List: List each media item you would include on this slide/page.

Images: filenames _____ , _____

Sounds: filenames _____ , _____

Video/Animation/Other: _____ , _____

Multimedia Storyboard

MENU SLIDE/PAGE

Write your slide/page title here . . .

Write your topic titles here . . . (you might use the titles of your subsequent pages)

Media List: List each media item you would include on this slide/page.

Images: filenames _____ , _____

Sounds: filenames _____ , _____

Video/Animation/Other: _____ , _____

Multimedia Storyboard

CONTENT SLIDE/PAGE

Write your slide/page title here . . .

Media Stage:

Use this area to place graphics.

You can even use printed images. Simply "cut-and-paste" pictures you wish to use on this page here.

Scissors and Glue :)

Media Caption:

Write your slide/page content here . . .

Media List: List each media item you would include on this slide/page.

Images: filenames _____ , _____

Sounds: filenames _____ , _____

Video/Animation/Other: _____ , _____

Multimedia Storyboard

CONTENT SLIDE/PAGE

Write your slide/page title here . . .

Write your slide/page content here . . .

Media Stage:

Use this area to place graphics.

You can even use printed images. Simply "cut-and-paste" pictures you wish to use on this page here.

Scissors and Glue :)

Media Caption:

Media List: List each media item you would include on this slide/page.

Images: filenames _____ , _____

Sounds: filenames _____ , _____

Video/Animation/Other: _____ , _____

Multimedia Storyboard

CONCLUSION SLIDE/PAGE

Write your slide/page title here . . .

Write closing thoughts here . . .

Media List: List each media item you would include on this slide/page.

Images: filenames _____ , _____

Sounds: filenames _____ , _____

Video/Animation/Other: _____ , _____

Presentation Storyboard

Student Name: _____ Course # _____ Section # _____

| TITLE SLIDE |

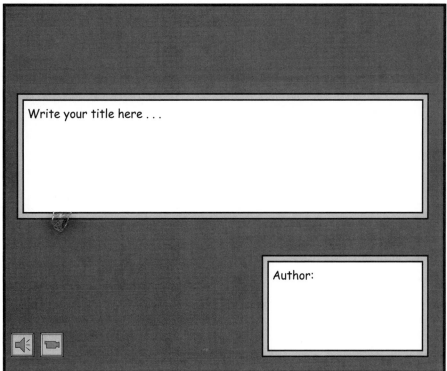

Slide Media List:

🔊 Sounds

Music _____

_____

Voice _____

_____

📹 Video _____

_____

_____

Other _____

_____

Notes:
_____
_____
_____
_____
_____
_____
_____
_____
_____
_____
_____
_____

Presentation Storyboard

OUTLINE SLIDE

Write your slide title here . . .

Write the titles of each slide or major points of your presentation below . . .

Notes:
_____
_____
_____
_____
_____
_____
_____
_____
_____
_____
_____
_____

Slide Media List:

🔊 Sounds
Music _____
_____

Voice _____
_____

📷 Video _____
_____
_____

Other _____
_____

Presentation Storyboard

CONTENT SLIDE

Write your slide title here . . .

Image Area:
Pictures and clip-art are placed here.

Cut-and-paste an image here.

Or list file name:
_____

Bullets: Write key points below . . .

Notes:

_____
_____
_____
_____
_____
_____
_____
_____
_____
_____
_____
_____
_____

Slide Media List:

🔊 Sounds

Music _____
_____

Voice _____
_____

📹 Video _____
_____
_____

Other _____
_____

Presentation Storyboard

CONTENT SLIDE

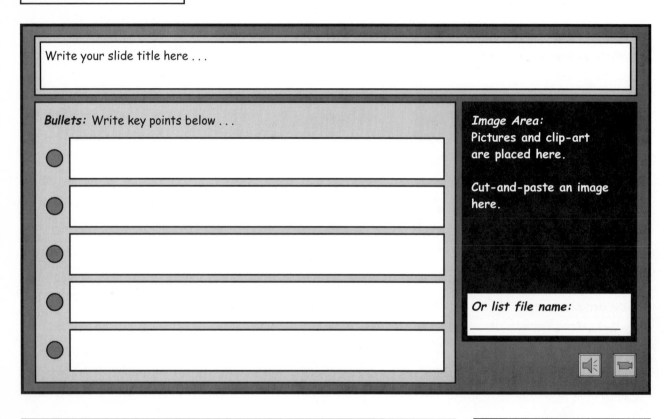

Write your slide title here . . .

Bullets: Write key points below . . .

Image Area:
Pictures and clip-art are placed here.

Cut-and-paste an image here.

Or list file name:

Notes:

Slide Media List:

🔊 Sounds
Music _____

Voice _____

📹 Video _____

Other _____

Presentation Storyboard

CONTENT SLIDE

Write your slide title here . . .

Bullets: Write key points below . . .

Bullets: Write key points below . . .

Notes:

_____
_____
_____
_____
_____
_____
_____
_____
_____
_____
_____

Slide Media List:

🔊 Sounds
Music _____

_____

Voice _____

_____

📹 Video _____

_____

_____

Other _____

_____

Presentation Storyboard

CONTENT SLIDE

Write your slide title here . . .

Image Area: Place Pictures and clip-art here.

Image Area: Place Pictures and clip-art here.

Or list file name: _____

Or list file name: _____

Bullets: Write key points below . . .

Notes:

_____
_____
_____
_____
_____
_____
_____
_____
_____
_____
_____
_____

Slide Media List:

Sounds
Music _____
_____
Voice _____
_____
Video _____
_____
_____
Other _____
_____

Presentation Storyboard

CONTENT SLIDE

Write your slide title here . . .

Bullets: Write key points below . . .

Notes:
_____
_____
_____
_____
_____
_____
_____
_____
_____
_____
_____
_____

Slide Media List:

Sounds
Music _____
_____

Voice _____
_____

Video _____
_____

Other _____
_____

Companion Web Site Storyboard

COURSE WELCOME PAGE

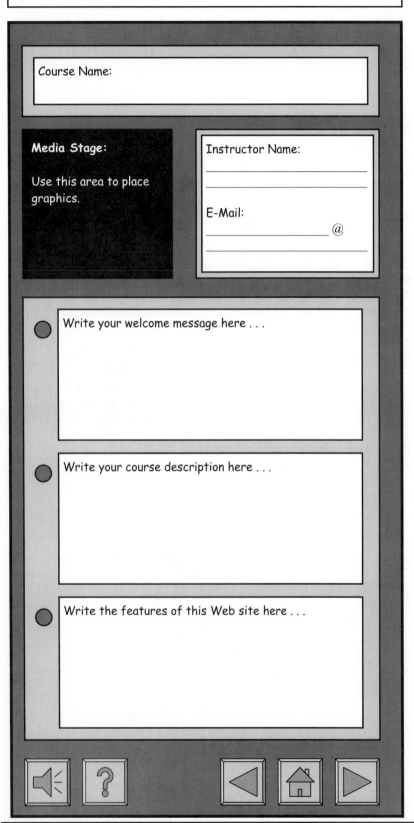

As Web sites become more complex, creating storyboards to plan them is becoming a more common practice. The next few pages provide you with templates you can use with students to make a blueprint for a potential Web site.

The welcome message should consist of a single sentence greeting visitors to your Web site.

The course description should be a brief paragraph summarizing the topics covered in this course.

The Web features section should list any special resources found at this Web site.

Companion Web Site Storyboard

COURSE DESCRIPTION PAGE

The course description should consist of a brief description of the course's subject matter, textbook and course materials information, a calendar of events, special announcements, and assignments and grading criteria .

Companion Web Site Storyboard

COURSE CONTACT PAGE

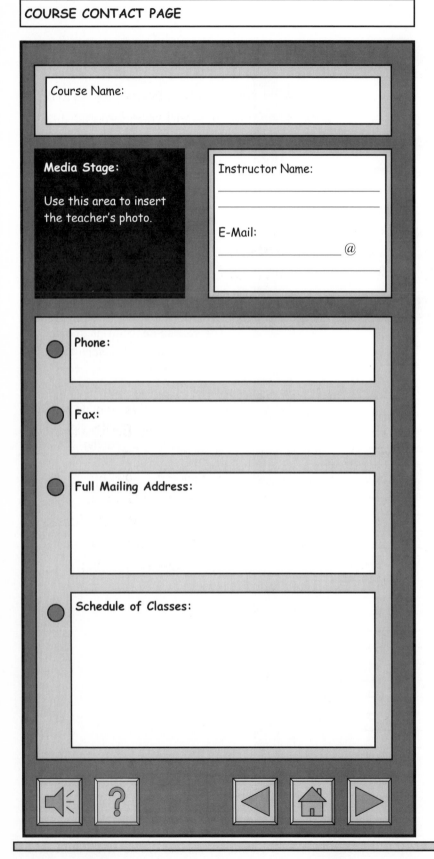

Course Name:

Media Stage:

Use this area to insert the teacher's photo.

Instructor Name:

E-Mail:

@

Phone:

Fax:

Full Mailing Address:

Schedule of Classes:

Enter your work phone number including area code.

Enter your work fax number including area code.

Enter your full work mailing address including your office or classroom location.

Enter your schedule of classes indicating any planning or "free" periods.

About This Workbook and CD-ROM

About the Authors

Joseph H. Howell is currently the Director of Instructional Technology at Pensacola Junior College. He received a Ph.D. in the Humanities from Florida State University. Prior to his current position he served as Professor of History and the Humanities at Gulf Coast Community College for 10 years. He has authored several books and software titles. His special interests include the design and delivery of interactive Web software.

Stephen W. Dunnivant is currently the Coordinator of Instructional Technology Design at Gulf Coast Community College. He holds a Master's degree in Educational Technology Leadership from George Washington University. A former K-12 instructor, he is the co-developer of multimedia student authoring software and is also active in the design of educational Web sites.

Acknowledgements

We wish to thank the following individuals for their contributions to this project: Dr. John Phillips of Gulf Coast Community College and Michael Dunnivant of Bay District Schools for their guest articles; Beth Kaufmann and Terri Wise of McGraw-Hill College Division for their editorial direction; and Cellestine Cheeks of Towson University, T. Kaye Abight of Missouri Southern State College, Denise Schmidt of Iowa State University, Neal Strudler of the University of Nevada Las Vegas, James L. Murphy of Elon College, Sarah Huyvaert of Eastern Michigan University, and Norman Sterchele of Saginaw Valley State University for their reviews of this project.